WHEN LIGHTNING STRUCK!

WHEN
LIGHTNING

STRUCK!

The Story of Martin Luther

Danika Cooley

Fortress Press
Minneapolis

Cover design: Brad Norr
Book design: PerfecType, Nashville, TN

Library of Congress Cataloging-in-Publication Data is available
Print ISBN: 978-1-5064-0583-4
eISBN: 978-1-5064-0630-5

The paper used in this publication meets the minimum requirements of
American National Standard for Information Sciences — Permanence
of Paper for Printed Library Materials, ANSI Z329.48-1984.

Manufactured in the U.S.A.

With love for
Ed
Erik, Forrest, and Amber
Tyson and Adalyn

— ∎ —

And sincere gratitude to
Chip MacGregor
April McGowan
Cendrine Hosoda
Bill and Barbie Johnson

CONTENTS

Chapter 1

THUNDERSTORM!

July 2, 1505

Martin Luther's leggings felt hot and oppressive against his skin in the stagnant heat, and his dark hair slicked wet against his forehead. The Saxon village of Stotternheim sat upon the horizon, a welcome sight after the young man's fifty-mile walk from the home of his parents in Mansfeld. Martin's destination, the University of Erfurt, was only about a mile past the medieval town—just beyond the lakes ahead.

A quick burst of wind stirred the dust from the road, pelting Martin's student tunic with a fine coating of chalky brown silt. Martin furrowed his brow and stood in the road for a moment, examining the sky. Dark clouds churned like angry dragons nipping at each other's heels. *A storm's coming.* The university student quickened his steps, adjusting his heavy purple cloak as he marched. The cape was secured around an expensive set of Latin law books his father had given him on his ten-day visit home.

Martin allowed his thoughts to wander as he hurried toward the ancient hamlet of Stotternheim. He smiled as he thought of the wealthy young woman his mother had found to be his wife once he finished school.

Overhead the heavens roiled and growled, reminding Martin of his precarious situation—exposed on the open road under a turbulent sky. Martin glanced upward and bit his lip. Black clouds crowded the sun from sight, making the noon hour appear to be dusk. He wondered what fight or mischief might be occurring in the spiritual realm to create such impending chaos here on earth. For Martin, witches and goblins were as real as angels and demons. When the sky snarled, he knew there must be trouble in heaven above.

The future lawyer paused to wipe the sweat from his brow. Fat raindrops fell to the hot dirt road at the law student's feet, sending up little puffs of dry dust. Nothing was truly mundane in Martin's life, and he wondered if the coming storm was God's way of speaking to him. *Perhaps God is not pleased with my life choices. Will God accept me when I die? Have I worked hard enough for my salvation?* In his heart, Martin knew he would not see heaven as a lawyer. After all, the teachings of the church were clear: the only way to truly serve God did not involve Martin's expensive books and lofty career.

Quickening his steps, Martin resolved to reach the out-lying buildings of Stotternheim before the storm broke in earnest. The long grass on either side of the road lay nearly flat in the strengthening gales of wind. Suddenly the black-ened sky lit up as a tongue of lightning licked the hori-zon like flames from the mouth of an irate serpent. Craggy rocks glittered in flashes of white fire.

Martin began to run, clutching his schoolbooks. He gripped the hilt of his sword with his opposite hand. A pro-tective weapon was a necessity on the open road. His foot-steps fell harder and swifter. Even German schoolchildren knew it was dangerous to be caught in a storm, and Martin was no stranger to death. As rain began to hit the road in torrents, the frantic student squinted and searched for shel-ter. His toe hit a stone and Martin faltered, swinging the blade of his sword wide with one hand, throwing the other arm beneath himself for protection.

Martin hit the ground and rolled, then clambered to his feet. He could feel the wrathful hiss of the sky as the earth shook with the force of each clap of thunder. It was as if a giant was barreling down the road, intent on crush-ing Martin beneath his heavy footfall. With every passing moment, the blazing lightning struck closer and the thun-der exploded louder, reverberating through his body.

Martin forced himself to concentrate on the ragged rhythm of his feet hitting the ground. The precious law books wrapped within his soaked purple cloak weighed him down as the wind and rain pelted his face. Above him, the atmosphere bellowed and roared. Martin was certain that this kind of rage could only come from God in heaven.

Spying an elm tree ahead of him, Martin veered off the road. Long, sprouted grass whipped at his leggings. Stumbling over ruts and stones, Martin threw his books toward the trunk of the tree and skidded to a stop beneath its leaves. He crouched doubled over with his hands above his knees and stared out into the storm. *I am safe!* The young man's chest heaved like a wounded beast seeking one final breath of life-giving air.

Out of the furious firmament came a thunderclap so loud, Martin was certain he heard God's voice shouting at him. At precisely the same moment, a bolt of lightning hit the elm tree above. The leaves and trunk of the tree burst into flames, throwing Martin to the ground.

Flinging his arms over his face in terror, Martin rolled on his back like a defeated knight fending off the inferno of an encroaching dragon. His eyes were blinded in the blaze of light. Martin was certain now that God was indeed speaking to him—and God was angry. *What can I do to fend off such a God—a God of lightning and thunder, a God of judgment? Certainly I cannot approach Him on my own!* "Saint Anna, help me!" he screamed, calling to the patron saint of miners. "I will become a monk!"

Chapter 2

THE DARK BEFORE DAWN

1483–1497

Martin lay reeling and blind on the ground in the midst of the terrible storm. His life now promised to God as a monk, his years as a child and a student seemed to play out before him.

■ ■ ■

Martin's stubby four-year-old fingers brushed aside brown, wet leaves until he found a fallen branch. With great care, he added it to the small bundle of sticks he held in his arms. The boy winced as the movement pulled skin against a thick scab that snaked across his hand—a constant reminder of

5

Martin's foolishness the day before. He'd been hungry, but it was not yet time for dinner. On impulse the child had grabbed a nut from a bowl on the family's trestle table. In a rage, Martin's mother, Margaretha, had grabbed his wrist and, holding him tightly, struck his pudgy little hand with a long stick until the blood ran down his arm.

Today the wound throbbed red and sore.

The sound of Margaretha's voice prodded the little boy onward. His mother moved deftly through the woods ahead of him, thrusting large pieces of fallen wood into the cloth slung across her back while singing a Thuringian folk song. "If folk don't like you and me, the fault with us is like to be."[1]

"Mother," interrupted Martin. "Why did the baby die? I thought I was to have a brother."

Margaretha turned, peering at Martin from beneath her tented linen head covering. Her deep-set eyes were darkly shadowed below the headdress. It seemed to Martin that the rounded point at the end of her chin matched the circular knob that was the tip of her nose. "It was that neighbor of ours. She is a witch, if I ever saw one. A witch is the reason my baby died."

Martin slipped on a pile of wet leaves and nearly dropped his sticks. The young boy remembered days ago the brand-new little fingers wrapped around his dirty thumb. He frowned in frustration and anger over the lost promise of a new playmate.

Just last month, the cheerful neighbor down the road had given him a handful of cherries and asked him about the baby, soon to be born. "Share with your mother, little one." She had smiled. "She'll be needing some good food these last weeks." Confusion clouded Martin's mind.

"Mother? How do you know our neighbor is a witch?"

Margaretha Luther narrowed her dark eyes. "Of course she's a witch. I know a witch when I see one." She kicked aside a pile of leaves and bent to pull up a large, rotten root. "'Twas a good thing Papa had my boy baptized right after he was born." She won her battle with the root and tucked it into her cloth sling.

Martin wrinkled his nose as he thought, stuffing two more sticks into the bulging bundle beneath his arm. "Mother, did Papa take me to be baptized after I was born?"

"Oh, yes, Martin, he did. Baptism is the only way to be sure a baby will make it to heaven if they die." She looked past Martin, her face softening. "So many babies die. Most of them, in fact." Margaretha shook her head as though she were trying to shed water from her hair. "No matter. Martin," she wagged her crooked finger at the little boy, "it was our duty to see you baptized. Your father set out the morning after your birth."

Margaretha continued rummaging beneath low bushes for fallen tree branches as she and Martin wound their way through the woods back toward the town of Mansfeld. "'Twas the feast of Saint Martin, so you were named after the holy saint. Your father, he took you down the street to Saint Peter's Church, to the lower tower room. That was the only part of the church that had been built." Margaretha looked back at Martin. "That was when we lived in Eisleben, you know."

Martin nodded at his mother. "You and Papa moved so that he could mine copper here in Mansfeld, right, Mother?"

"That's right, Martin. Step carefully through this creek, son. Mind you don't tread on any water sprites." Martin picked his way through the water on his tiptoes, pausing on a large, flat rock to bend at the waist and peer into the stream, searching for fairies. The sticks in his arms weighed on his little body and he rocked back and forth before steadying himself. Martin squinted, but was unable to see any of the magical creatures he was supposed to avoid. His sore hand throbbed and he righted his stance, hurrying after his mother before she could notice he was lagging behind.

On the trip home, Martin thought about what his mother had said. He was glad that his baby brother had gone to heaven. Martin didn't really understand the rules about who could enter heaven, just as he did not understand how his kind neighbor could be responsible for the death of his brother. Yet, Martin decided his mother would not lie. Surely she was afraid—of hell, of water sprites and witches, of breaking the rules of the church. If someone as wise as his mother was afraid, Martin believed he had reason to fear as well.

— ■ —

"Martin!" When the Latin teacher at the Mansfeld school said Martin's name, it always had a harsh, scraping tone to it, like the sound of picks hitting copper in the mines outside Mansfeld.

"Yes, Sir." Martin was careful to speak only in Latin, never in German. He fought to pull himself back from his daydreams.

"We will hear the *Confiteor* now."

Martin stood and stared at the wall ahead of him. At age six, he had already attended school for a year and a half. Latin would one day come easily to Martin. For now, he still thought in German. He cleared his throat and began his confession in a clear, sweet voice:

> I confess to almighty God,
> to the Blessed Mary, ever virgin,
> to the Blessed Peter and to all the Saints and unto you
>   brothers
> I have sinned,
> my fault
> I pray that you pray for me.[2]

Martin settled on his stool, thinking about the words of the *Confiteor* as the student next to him rose to recite the Lord's Prayer in Latin. *I wonder why we ask the saints to pray for us,* thought Martin. *Why is it that we do not pray to God ourselves? Father says the saints have stored up good deeds, like the farmer down the road stores barley for winter. How can it be that our good deeds are able to be stored?*

"Jürgen!" snapped the teacher. The unhappy student next to Martin had lapsed into German midway through the Lord's Prayer. "You are speaking in German! You are the Donkey!" Martin cringed as the Wolf, the student responsible for spying on the others, jumped to his feet and rushed to remove a wooden donkey mask from the face of one of the youngest boys in the class. With great ceremony, the Wolf placed the donkey mask on Jürgen's face before writing "Jürgen" on a slate with a wooden wolf on top.

Martin frowned. His name appeared on the slate fifteen times. That week, his assigned work had consisted of learning conjugations and declinations in Latin. Martin had been busy with chores around his home and he had failed to memorize the grammar he was expected to recite. With an unhappy resignation, the boy realized he could expect to receive fifteen whippings tomorrow morning—one beating for each time his name appeared on the slate that week. Deep within his chest, Martin felt the old familiar burn of resentment.

I hate the beatings and the donkey. If I ever have a son, I will never beat him, or humiliate him like my teacher or my father do. I will never make him walk so far to school each way when he is only four-and-a-half years old. If it hadn't been for Nicolaus Emler, an older boy who had carried him to and from school until Martin was old enough to walk the entire distance on his own, he never would have made it.

Although Martin hated being shamed into learning, he was bright and he grasped new information well. The growing boy did love how his schooling pleased his father. By the time Martin was thirteen, he knew that a decision would soon be made about his future.

■ ▪ ■

"Johann," Martin laughed loudly. "You mustn't say such things! Someone will overhear you, and we shall have to do penance."

Johann Reinecke's bright eyes sparkled. "Aren't you afraid that if we don't do penance, we will burn in hell—whether the baker hears us or not?"

Martin's smile vanished as he strode down the crooked dirt road through Mansfeld. He was careful to walk in the center of the street, far from the upper windows of the stucco-covered brick homes and shops lining the road where the inhabitants emptied buckets of refuse in a dirty cascade to the gutters below. Wild dogs and pigs roamed the streets, searching beneath garbage for a meal. In the dark alleys, colonies of rats awaited nightfall, when they would begin their feasting. Beyond the walls of the city lay the thick forest where Martin still gathered firewood for his mother. The Latin student glanced behind himself at the church square down the crooked, narrow main street. The massive castle and church stood side by side next to the school on a raised bed of land. Martin had walked this road to and from school for ten years now.

At thirteen, Martin was nearly a man. He was quick-witted, with a tongue sharp enough to carve diamonds. He wondered if his cynical friend was correct about the perilous nature of their fate. How could he possibly do enough to please the Judge who would decide his eternal destiny? "Perhaps if we follow the rules of the church, if we see enough relics, make a pilgrimage, and do our penance well," Martin said as he paused in thought for a moment. "Maybe then we'll see heaven after purgatory."

Johann kicked at a stray cat. "Maybe we will go to heaven, Martin. But there's no way to truly know, is there?"

Martin grimaced and shrugged. "I suppose not. Even if we do go to heaven, we can expect to spend thousands—or millions—of years being tortured in purgatory first." The pensive student sighed. Salvation from his sins seemed like such an impossible prize to hope for. Yet, Martin did hope.

The boys parted as Martin made his way into the courtyard of his family's small, two-room cottage near the city wall. Hens clawed the yard, searching for scraps of food. From within the cottage, Martin could hear the hungry cries of his six younger brothers and sisters.

Martin's father, Hans, loomed in the doorway. The man had a formidable bearing, his heavy brow creased and his thin lips drawn into a contemplative frown. In the twelve years since the Luthers had moved to Mansfeld, Hans had progressed from working in the copper mines to leasing a mine of his own. Martin knew that it was through hard work and courage that his father had worked his way from the dangerous underground caverns, becoming a respected business owner. Others in the town had observed Hans's character, and the serious mine owner had served as one of Mansfeld's four councilmen for six years now.

Hans was strict; he once beat Martin so severely that the boy fled from home, not intending to return. Upon realizing the error of alienating his brilliant and promising first-born son, Hans had run after Martin to beg his forgiveness. Martin remembered his father's sincere apology with affectionate wonder. The boy took note of the fact that in spite of all his harsh expectations, Hans still knelt beside Martin every evening to pray for his eldest son. If there was one person in the world Martin wished to please, it was his father.

"Martin. It is time to leave." Hans's frown deepened and the crease above his nose took on the look of a narrow chasm.

Martin could feel his confusion draw the features of his face together like storm clouds gathering before a rain burst. "Leave? Where are we to go, Father?"

Hans shook his head. "No, Martin. I am not going anywhere. You will travel with Johann tomorrow to Magdeburg to attend the school there under the Brethren of the Common Life, so that one day you can attend law school. Your mother and I intend for you to care for our needs once you find work as a lawyer." Hans nodded, as if reassuring himself.

"Father—Where will I stay? What will I eat?" Martin felt a dark storm of panic rush over him. Though he walked to school on his own, the young man had not been outside of Mansfeld, and certainly he had not traveled or provided for his own needs.

"You will stay with the Brothers at the monastery," Hans said. "You will find your own food; you may sing for your dinner as the other students do. Mother will send a loaf of bread with you in the morning. You must leave early, Martin—Magdeburg is forty miles away and it will take you several days to reach the city."

Hans spun on his heel and disappeared into the cottage, leaving Martin standing in the waning light, chickens pecking at his feet.

Chapter 3

BEGGING FOR BREAD

1497–1502

Martin and his friends laughed loudly as they trudged down the streets of Magdeburg, where they attended the school of the Brethren of the Common Life.

"Johann!" Martin was jubilant that particular evening and he elbowed his friend playfully. "We've never caroled this far out toward the edge of the city before! Look, the Elbe River lies before us, just past those buildings." Martin considered Magdeburg's history of sieges and wondered why it was not protected by a strong stone wall, as Mansfeld was.

Johann wrapped his cloak tighter against the frigid air, shivering with nervous energy. "That farmhouse over there is all alone, Martin. Perhaps they will share more than a slice of bread with us; it is almost Christmas, after all." Johann's voice cracked a little.

"Of course they will, Johann!" Martin slapped his friend on the back. "Who would not want to feed such a handsome band of young singers?"

As they approached the home, the boys began to slow, their trepidation over the house's isolation mounting.

"That house looks rather foreboding," said one of the students. "We are right at the edge of town, are we not? Perhaps we are now outside of Magdeburg. After all, who would put a farm inside a city?"

"There's really no one else around here," commented another. "And the farmhouse is rundown—perhaps no one lives here at all."

Martin looked about him. The Elbe River ran silent, a wide chasm of dark water. On the other side, green fields were dotted with spots of forest. To Martin's left and right, woodlands crept across the fields toward the town, like predators on the hunt. Behind the boys there was a stretch of land before houses began to appear closer and closer together until the little town flowed into the central market where the cathedral stood, spires missing like a bull with its horns sawed off. Martin knew that the townspeople had set about rebuilding the church when it burnt to the ground some three hundred years before. All that remained to construct were the tall spires that graced the other cathedrals across Germany. In the waning light Martin could just make out the archbishop's palace towering over the small homes and shops. He knew his school lay in the general direction of the two massive buildings. Throughout the small town churches and chapels squatted, ensuring that no citizen would be without spiritual counsel at any given time.

Martin turned back to his friends with a forced air of confidence. "Nonsense. I'm hungry, aren't you?" With that, he burst into song, a cheerful ballad about the birth of the Christ. The other boys joined in, their young voices singing loudly for the dinner they hoped to receive.

There was a loud crash from behind the small two-room hut, and a gruff, angry voice shouted, "I hear you boys. Show yourselves!"

Martin had never moved so quickly in his fourteen years. Within a breath, he was out of the dirt street, crouching behind a plum tree. Looking around, he could see no sign of his friends.

"Boys! Boys!" yelled the farmer in a deep, husky voice. "You must return, boys!" Scattering chickens as he ran around the corner of his home, a rough and portly man appeared, his hands laden with thick, homemade sausages. "Boys! You did not finish your song!"

Martin laughed uproariously and crawled out from behind the tree. "Friends, our farmer here bears gifts for your Christmas!" Martin stood and began to sing once again. One by one, his friends crept from their hiding places to join the chorus. When they finished their songs, the farmer smiled a toothless grin between cracked and weathered lips and handed each a misshapen sausage.

On the way back into town, the boys sang at several additional houses, receiving mugs of steaming apple cider and hunks of thick, dark bread. As they neared the marketplace, Martin noticed a thin man moving slowly from door to door, his spine bent downward near the center like a reed that has broken in the wind and then healed, leaving it crooked and gnarled at the joint.

"Johann, do you see that man? He looks to be a death's head, mere bone and skin. He carries that sack like a donkey bent under a heavy load.[1] What is he doing, and why does he do it?"

Johann glanced at the tortured man, wincing slightly at the sight. "That is Prince William of Anhalt." His voice sounded bored and unaffected. "His brother is the bishop of Merseburg. Prince William has taken the vow of a monk, and he fasts and prays until he looks to be a living skeleton. Right now he is begging bread for his brothers in the monastery, as is his usual habit."

Martin gasped as the prince-turned-monk extended his bone-thin arm to knock on the door of a nearby home. Prince William looked just like Martin's nightmares of a skeleton come to life. His skin was paper-thin and stretched oddly across his joints. "Why? Why does he do this?"

"Well, to go to heaven, of course," shrugged Johann. "He is earning his salvation, though the man will still need to go to purgatory first. But becoming a monk like Prince William and denying the pleasures of this world is the only sure way of salvation."

"The only sure way to heaven is to live as that man? Perhaps, then, I will never be saved. Whoever looks at him must be ashamed of his own worldly position."[2] Martin could feel the joy from earlier in the evening seeping from his body and pooling into puddles on the surface of the earth. He felt the cold of the season take root in his soul.

Martin returned to school that evening with a full belly and a troubled heart. *How, exactly, can I find my way to heaven and work hard enough to guarantee that God will accept me? If Prince William is unable to avoid the torture of purgatory, how could a wealthy lawyer—as I hope to be—ever please God?*

Martin sang door to door for his supper throughout the year he attended the school of the Brethren of the Common Life. It was during a break between classes that Martin began to visit the school library, looking earnestly through the books chained to the tables.

Books in medieval Germany were expensive and Martin was just a boy from a peasant family with a father who mined copper, so he hadn't seen many written works. Though Martin had heard of a marvelous machine called the printing press, designed by a man named Johann Gutenberg nearly sixty years before, the books in the library were all clearly handwritten, with faint lines beneath each row of elaborate lettering. He breathed deeply the smell of parchment as he walked up and down the rows of tables. Each book lay closed on the flat surfaces, chained to the wood. Martin moved down the tables until he found an open book. He fingered one of the chains while examining a magnificently illustrated page in front of him. A large, open M at the top of the page contained an entire scene with a shepherd and his sheep. An extensive border consisting of scrolling lines and pictures of people and animals surrounded the page, accented by gold leafing. The effect was breathtaking.

Surely the chains exist to prevent the theft of such marvelous works of art! I wonder if the newly machine-printed books have colors and pictures such as these. The man we learned of in class yesterday—Cristóbal Colón, I think his name was, who returned by ship from a new world just five years ago—I wonder if he found books such as these in the new land?

Martin continued examining the dusty Latin volumes bound in leather along the tables when he came upon another thick work lying open. Strong parchment pages held elaborate, rounded black lettering in two even columns. A large ornate letter like the one in the first book signaled the beginning of the Latin words. Colorful scrolled vines, flowers, and a strangely elongated woman holding a long, thin baby meandered down the page between the two rows of words, accented with gold leaf. Drawn to the splendid pages by a force Martin could never have resisted, he began to read aloud:

> *Now there was a certain man of Ramathaimzophim, of mount Ephraim, and his name was Elkanah, the son of Jeroham, the son of Elihu, the son of Tohu, the son of Zuph, an Ephrathite: And he had two wives; the name of the one was Hannah, and the name of the other Peninnah: and Peninnah had children, but Hannah had no children.*[3]

Martin was mesmerized. He continued to read through the story of Hannah, a woman who begged the Lord for a son. The poor woman wanted a baby so badly, she promised to dedicate the child to God. He read of the birth of little

Samuel, Hannah's first baby. In wonder, Martin learned that Hannah had taken young Samuel to the temple to live with the priest Eli.

Smoothing the hair off his forehead with the palm of his hand, Martin sighed aloud. *I have never heard this story. Look at how grand this book is! There must be many more stories . . . Oh, how I wish that I could have a Bible of my own.*

Martin jumped at the sound of the library clock striking the new hour. He hurried out the door to his next class, casting a backward glance at the book he would spend his life studying. Over the following months, Martin visited the school library often, always returning to read the fascinating stories in the Bible.

＊＊＊

One year after he began school at Magdeburg, Martin's father moved him to a new institute in Eisenach.

Martin filed into class on his first day, joking with the young men around him. At the front of the room, Master Trebonius stood and swept off his hat with regal ceremony. "I offer my services to those who will one day serve our Lord and our great Germany as future mayors, chancellors, learned doctors, and rulers; although you do not know them now, it is proper that you should show them honor!"[4] Martin grinned in delight. It seemed his experience in Eisenach would be nothing like his younger school years. Master Trebonius of Eisenach's School of Saint George the Dragon Slayer insisted that his students be treated with respect and dignity.

Eisenach was only ten miles from Martin's home in Mansfeld. Here Martin had relatives on his mother's side, but he was responsible for securing his own housing and food. Martin excelled at Latin and at caroling. In singing for his supper door to door, he had endeared himself to Ursula Cotta, a joyous German woman married to Kunz, a wealthy businessman. Kunz and Ursula had taken Martin into their four-story brick home on George Street to live, sending him to eat meals with their relatives, Heinrich Schalbe and his family.

As soon as Master Trebonius released his students for the day, Martin moved happily through the halls of the decrepit and crumbling school building into the paved streets. Stretching, he eyed the massive Wartburg Castle that crouched on a hill far above the stone walls around the city. The bulwark of the Wartburg extended to either side of the keep, the strong tall tower overlooking the town. The wood-framed apartment windows, carved into the stone structure, glared at Martin as a hundred scheming eyes. *She looks almost like a dragon herself, ready to pounce on some poor unsuspecting monk!*

Martin hurried to the Schalbe home where little Henry met him at the door. "Hello, Martin!" the boy said. "I'm ready for my lesson. Father says that if I learn my Latin well, I can go to market with Mother. Can we hurry? Will you tell Father I did well? Do you think I'm learning?"

"Wait, Henry." Martin laughed at the eager child. "We will begin right away, but you cannot rush Latin! Let's see how well you remember yesterday's lesson. Perhaps if you do well, you can go with your mother, and I can sit and listen to your father's guests."

"Why do you want to listen to a bunch of monks?" asked Henry, wrinkling his forehead.

"I like listening to the monks. But your father's guests tonight may not be monks. It could happen that he will entertain another artist, a few musicians, or even a priest." Martin's eyes sparkled at the thought of sitting in the room with such distinguished individuals, learning about Renaissance culture and society. Maybe he would even be allowed to play his lute again. He would ask Frau Schalbe if he could play from the piece he had written earlier that week.

Henry burst into Martin's thoughts again. "I can see why you like the artists and the musicians, but why would you care about what a monk or a priest has to say? If you want to see one, you can just stand on the street. There are so many churchmen in Eisenach. Sometimes I think there are more priests here than children!"

"Henry, I like to listen to the priests talk about how we can earn our way to heaven. I want to go to heaven one day, don't you? I don't want to forget any of the rules we must follow."

Henry shrugged. "Martin, my father says that I disobey so often, I'll be in purgatory for at least a million years. I don't think a thousand years here or there will matter too much."

Martin's eyes widened in surprise. He clapped his younger friend and student on the back. "I wish I had your confidence, Henry. Come; let's get started on your Latin before you miss bartering at the market with your mother."

— ■ —

Martin spent three years in Eisenach, tutoring Henry, pol-
ishing his Latin, and listening to the town's many monks
and priests speak of heaven and hell in the dining hall of
Heinrich Schalbe. Martin's after-hours education, when his
thoughts turned to the divine, would have an impact that
no one could have predicted. In just a few years, Martin
Luther would have a lot to say about what the Bible teaches
about God, sin, salvation, heaven and hell—and the things
Martin Luther had to say would change the world.

Chapter 4

THE EDGE OF DEATH

1503

Martin groaned and threw his arm over his face as the ringing of the church bell reverberated through his chest. Resigning himself to face the brisk morning air, Martin placed his feet on the cold stone floor of his dormitory.

A froggy voice next to Martin taunted him. "What's the matter, Philosopher? Is it too early for you?"

"Not at all, friend," Martin said as he pulled his student tunic over his head. "I quite enjoy the winter. After all, I would much rather rise at 6 AM than 4 AM. It's just a bit drafty in here—I'm glad for our robes."

In the bed across from Martin, a lump in the blanket moved. "Hieronymus, wake up man!" Martin shook the lump violently. "You can't be late again. Remember the last time? Rector Trutvetter will have your head. Out of bed, you slothful pig of a boy!"

Martin looked up to see six of his friends stifling laughter. One of them lit a lantern by the door and soft light played across the snow blowing in through the open window. Martin placed a finger to his lips and stepped to his cot, pulling his lute from beneath his cot. Leaning over the lump that was Hieronymus, Martin strummed a jovial dancing tune aimed right above the spot where he judged his friend's ear to be.

Hieronymus shot out of bed with a yell. "They're coming! I tell you, they're coming! Run. We must run!"

Martin and his friends doubled over in laughter. "So the lazy sow awakens at last! What are you dreaming of, Hieronymus? Knights and dragons, perhaps?"

Hieronymus glared at Martin, yanked his robe over his head, and started for the door.

Martin cleared his throat. "I apologize, friend. I had no idea that would frighten you so. I meant only to keep you from being late. You may want to reverse your tunic, though, or when you're coming, we'll all think you're going." He slapped his leg, laughing again with his dorm mates. This time, Hieronymus laughed as well, quickly turning his tunic around and blowing out the lantern.

"I'm not missing breakfast again, Martin. The master of the house doesn't give us enough time to eat as it is."

Martin slapped his close friend on the back. "Mr. Buntz, that is because you eat three times your fair share."

Hieronymus raised one eyebrow and cocked his head. "That is only because I love gruel. I can't get enough of the gray slop!" At that, all the boys laughed and rushed toward the kitchen. Already, they had nearly missed their meal. Not one dared be late to class.

The boys ran down the dark stone hallways to the kitchen before collapsing into their chairs. The master of the house gave them a hard look before turning to Martin.

"Martin, I hear you have a debate today."

"Yes, Housemaster, I do."

"What is the topic?"

"Syllogism, sir. I am debating Master Trutvetter. I will be defending Aristotle; the rector will be representing Buridan thought."

Hieronymus crowed from the far end of the long trestle table. "The mighty Philosopher takes on his rector and master in a battle of words. He may well slay you as Saint George slew the dragon, young Philosopher Luther!"

Martin laughed. After an acidic look from the housemaster, he glared at the rough wood of the table. The housemaster would ultimately decide whether Martin would advance to the final exams for his Master's degree, and the master's student could not afford to upset him.

The housemaster cleared his throat. "Martin, will you please say the table blessing? Herr Buntz can then read from Scripture for us."

Martin stood and recited the Latin prayer from memory: "Oh, Lord, bless us and these your gifts which from your bounty we are about to receive through Christ our Lord. Amen."

— ■ —

"Are you ready, Hieronymus?" called twenty-year-old Martin. Early-morning light poured in through the stone opening in their dorm room as Martin fastened his sword over his tunic, then pulled on his heavy cape. He shivered in the cool mid-April air.

"Ja," replied Hieronymus. "I could not be more ready to leave for home. This break has been well earned. If I never hear the name of Aristotle again, I shall be pleased. In fact, I may just stay home and become a farmer like my uncle."

Martin laughed. "You will be a rich lawyer, just like me." The young men made it to the stairs at the base of their dorm before Martin placed a hand on Hieronymus's forearm. "You have forgotten your sword, and I have forgotten my lute." They returned quickly to their room. Martin slung his stringed instrument over his back. He loved to play for his family. In fact, if Hans Luther had not insisted that Martin become a lawyer, he might have chosen the path of a musician. However, the sword Hieronymus had forgotten was vital. No German student would be foolish enough to travel the woods without protection. Martin shifted impatiently as Hieronymus strapped the sheath of his sword to his belt. "Come, let's march. I have farther to go than you."

The two friends set out on their journey home, agreeing to hike at least the first part together. Martin's feet hit the newly paved, crushed-stone streets of the city outside the University of Erfurt with a soft crunch at each step. He gazed about him at the steeples and spires down every lane.

On the highest hill an impressive cathedral loomed toward the icy sky. "Ah, you nest of priests." Martin stepped to his right, around the front of a stone building, only to travel back to his left to follow the path of the next storefront.

"Hieronymus, do you not think the city officials could have made the streets straight? Every building lies in a different place. I cannot see down the street, for there are shops and homes in my way at every step!"

Hieronymus laughed. "Friend, what do you expect of a place with only twenty thousand inhabitants to its twenty-four churches? Not to mention the dozens of monasteries, convents, and chapels? Then there is that monstrosity." Hieronymus gestured to the cathedral atop the hill. Martin gazed at the structure as his friend continued to tick off facts on his fingers, pink with cold. "Add to those all the hospitals the church controls—six! And, Martin, more than one hundred buildings for religious purposes!"

Martin cocked his head. "Did you count them?"

"Did I count what?"

"All those buildings?"

Hieronymus kicked a stone aside with his toe. "What else am I to do whilst you and Professor Trutvetter debate? Of course I counted them. In here." The student tapped his skull with a closed fist, winking and nodding at the same time.

"Why, you swine of a man! Perhaps you should be a farmer after all."

Hieronymus pursed his lips, serious for a moment. "Of course I should be. You are correct. You're right about this being a nest of priests as well."

Hieronymus paused on a footbridge crossing the stream running through the university's buildings. "Play a song for us, Martin. It will give us vigor for the journey!"

Martin played a strong, sad melody across the strings as he envisioned a great battle in the air about him. Swords flashed and clanked, horse's hooves clattered, and armor creaked. He could almost feel the heat of battle pressing in on him.

"Do you think Satan is stalking us even now?" he asked suddenly, dropping his lute to his side.

"What a thing to say. Why would that concern you?" Hieronymus frowned deeply. "Here we are in Little Rome, the center of the German church. We've graduated with bachelor's degrees, and we will soon arrive at our master's degrees. We study at a university promoted by the church, and your brilliant mind will one day rule legal battles, bringing you renown and riches. Yet, you are worried about Satan? I will never understand you."

"I heard it said in a lecture that Satan stalks like a lion. That he seeks to devour us. I hear Scripture calls him a dragon. I believe it to be true—it is what I have been taught since birth. Do you not think it is so?"

Hieronymus kicked a stone into the frigid water of the Gera River below. It bounced off the melting ice into the rushing current. "Oh, I believe he is stalking us. I'm just certain I am stronger."

Martin raised his eyebrow at his friend and chuckled in a nervous staccato. "That is a different perspective."

The young men continued on their way, winding through the uneven streets of the city, avoiding the many dead ends, and some less reputable areas. As university students, they were rarely outside of the supervision of the rector, the proctors, the master of the house, or the students who were employed to spy on their dorm mates. Martin breathed the freedom deeply through his nostrils and found that it stung his throat with chill.

As they neared the wall of the city, Martin gazed into the hills that rose above Erfurt. He imagined the slopes as they had looked in autumn. Fields planted in a dazzling array of colors to create indigo, blue, and yellow dyes had seemed to sway in time to Martin's lute. Erfurt was made rich by its dye trade as the colorful flowers brought with them wealth and prestige. Beyond the ascending fields, vineyards and orchards stretched into a thick forest. This early in the spring the trees and grapevines lay bare, miniature buds just beginning to form as leaves considered their debut appearance. The dirt beneath Martin's feet was slick and hard, still frozen at the end of a long winter.

"I can't wait to see Father," Martin enthused. "I think he will be pleased by the progress I have made in my schooling."

Hieronymus glanced sideways at Martin. "Pleasing your father is very important to you, isn't it, Martin?"

"Yes. My father is terribly strict—but I have great respect for him. When I am a lawyer, I will be able to support Father and Mother in their old age. But sometimes I wonder."

Martin stepped through a wide opening in the stone wall surrounding the city, nodding to the gatekeeper. Beneath his robe, his sword hung heavy against his leg—a reminder that dangers lay ahead in the woods. Martin doubted he could ever feel indestructible as Hieronymus did, able to take on a dragon.

When Martin did not speak again, Hieronymus prodded him. "What do you wonder, Philosopher? You think too much, I fear."

Martin sighed and worked backward through his memory to find his lost thread of thought. "It is true, I think too much. Yet, sometimes I'm concerned that a life as a lawyer is not what God would have for me. Am I doing enough to secure my salvation? For I am not certain that I can beat the dragon, Hieronymus—certainly not as a lawyer, concerned with wealth and prestige."

"Ja, Martin, you are hopeless." Hieronymus ran ahead. "Come, I'll race you to the forest."

Martin laughed and started off after his friend. Ice-laced wind pelted his face as his hood fell backward. For the moment, Martin forgot his fears of being stalked by Satan, or of falling short of God's expectations. Instead, he concentrated on the one thing he truly loved in life: winning. His footsteps fell hard and fast against the frozen ground as he raced through the barren fields. Past the grapevines he climbed, passing Hieronymus at the budding apple trees. By the end of the plum orchard, Martin was struggling to continue, his breath coming in ragged puffs. A streak of pain from a muscle in his side forced him to regulate his breath. He turned to see Hieronymus; perhaps he could slow his pace and still win.

Martin twisted, still running, and spied his fellow student amongst the plums, struggling to keep up. Slowing, he turned back toward the woods, determined to keep his slim lead. Martin's foot slipped against a rock with a sickening scraping sound. He wobbled and bobbed, fighting to keep himself upright. Throwing his arms to the side in an attempt to catch his balance, Martin brought his leg forward from behind and forced it up the hill, as his body sunk lower to the ground. Martin's lute slid across the icy dirt. The forest floor rose toward Martin like a bird taking flight.

It was too late to right himself. Martin plummeted to the frozen ground, landing hard upon his shoulder. Pain seared through him and he wretched against the dirt. Rolling to his back in agony, Martin gasped as he caught sight of his leg. The cold air filling his lungs caused him to sputter and wheeze, his chest constricting as if under a talon. Above Martin's knee, his sword protruded, waving in the air like a Crusader's flag.

"Saint Mary, help!" cried Martin as he grasped the hilt of his weapon and pulled it from his leg. The deep wound gaped clean, revealing a damaged and throbbing vein. He stared, appalled, his mind racing to take in the sight before he plunged his thumb into his leg. Finding the vein, he pressed with all his might.

Hieronymus puffed to the hilltop, white with horror as he stared wide-eyed down upon his friend. Blood spurted from Martin's leg, pooling on the hard ground. Martin could feel his flesh swelling against his hand, threatening to push his thumb from the nick in his vein. He struggled to keep his eyes open. As the world grew dark, over and over his lips mouthed, "Mary, help. Saint Mary, help."

Hieronymus whispered, "Forgive me," turned, and ran toward Erfurt, leaving his friend Martin in a pool of his own blood atop a hill overlooking the great German nest of priests.

Chapter 5

THE BLACK DEATH

1503–1505

M artin lay still against the ground, mouthing the words, "Help, Mary. Saint Mary, help me." The ground beneath him was frozen, and over time he lost feeling in his back. His swelling leg continued to press against his hand, growing taut with pressure, and sticky blood seeped through his fingers. Gradually, Martin lost feeling in his leg as well. The world above him became hazy as his life oozed from his wound.

"Ah, Satan, I knew you to be lurking," he rasped into the mist. "It looks as though you are in a good position to devour me, you old rogue. I am to lose this battle, and I know not where my soul will land. Will I even make it to purgatory? Ja, I hate losing."

Above Martin, the dim faces of his dorm mates wavered. "Ah, and now I have visions of my life. Soon, I suppose, my mother will be beating me with a cane stick for stealing a nut."

"He is delusional already." The far-off voice of Hieronymus seemed to swirl through Martin's soul. "Come. We must carry him; he cannot walk. Do not release that vein, Martin. If you lose hold of it, we cannot help you." Martin felt himself lifted from the ground. Above him twirled visions of spruces, plums, apples, and broad, ruddy faces red with effort.

Martin slipped in and out of consciousness as his friends hauled his dying body down the hill to the walls of the city. Clouds roiled through the dark sky above as he envisioned the prowling dragon roaring in anticipation and glee, awaiting its fading victim. Again, he heard the creaking of armor, the stamping of warhorses, and the clank of swords.

■■ ■ ■■

Martin put his hand to his forehead and groaned. His skin felt as though he was lying inside a furnace and his swollen eyes refused to open fully or focus clearly. Through the blur, Martin could see that Hieronymus slept slumped in a hard wooden chair beside Martin's straw mat. Outside the cell in which he lay, he could hear the deep male voices.

"Will he live?" Martin recognized the worry in his housemaster's voice.

"You've asked me this for two days now. I cannot tell you. By the color of his skin, I think not. His wound was deep, and he cut a main artery. I've sewed it up, but I cannot guarantee it will hold." Martin fought a wave of nausea as he wondered who the man speaking might be.

"Will he keep his leg?"

"Again, I cannot say. It is early still and we must wait."

There was a snort next to him, and Martin forced his gaze to focus on a blurry Hieronymus. Martin's friend sat up in his chair, frowning. "Ah, you are awake, friend." Hieronymus glanced toward the door. "Never mind the surgeon's words—what does he know? His job is sewing up pigs and sheep. Never before has he sewn up a Luther."

Martin groaned. His tongue felt thick in his mouth. "That is not comforting, man."

Hieronymus chuckled and blew out the lamp hanging from the wall before settling back into his chair. "Forget it and sleep. It's my night to watch you—I'll be right here if you need anything."

Martin sank back into a fitful slumber, his dreams filled with fire and dragons, battles and raging furnaces. Everywhere he turned the stink of old blood clung to the knight's tunic and leggings he wore. Ahead of him, Martin could see the retreating form of Mary, Jesus' mother. He chased after her, crying, "Mary, help," but she walked ahead, never stopping.

"Aahhh!" cried Martin, jolted from his fever. "Ahhh. It hurts, it hurts. Mary, why do you not help me?"

Hieronymus jumped from his chair, sending it crashing to the ground. He fumbled for the lamp before running into the hallway to call for help. Martin grabbed his leg, screaming in agony. His skin burned and great drops of sweat rolled down his face and chest.

Moments later, the small cell was filled with young men. A scruffy fellow pushed through the anxious students wielding a knife in the smoky light of the lamps swinging from the hands of Martin's friends.

"Hold him down! Quick—do not let him move. The artery has burst, and I must split his leg or we will lose him!"

Martin felt strong hands upon his calves, shoulders, and wrists. Too weak to struggle, he faded into the furnace of his dreams.

▬ ▪ ▬

Martin lived through his battle with his own sword. His artery was again sewn and eventually his fever waged war on infection. Slowly, he recovered enough to sit, to study, and to walk. Hieronymus Buntz was glad to see his friend restored, and life at the University of Erfurt continued on as it had before. Until, that is, the fiery serpent crouched and pounced, wiping out all in its path. It was still 1503 when terror reigned in Erfurt.

"Martin, Martin, wake up!" Hieronymus hissed, spit spraying from his lips.

"What do you want? It is the middle of the night!"

Martin could hear groaning and weeping coming from the hallway.

"Martin, it is here. The plague. The Black Death has come."

Martin gasped. The Black Death was known to kill without mercy, devouring all things living that stumbled into its reckless path.

The following months were spent caring for friends, and then burying their lifeless bodies. The sickening smell of death hung throughout the halls of the dormitory, in the lecture galleries, and through the streets of the city. By the time the plague appeared to tire of wreaking havoc on Erfurt, there was no one who had not buried a friend, a child, or a parent.

"Martin, never have I seen so much death." Hieronymus had darkened circles under his eyes. Martin thought he looked as though he had aged many years.

"Yes, it has been terrible. I cannot get the smell out of my nostrils. Never again will I call you a lazy pig. You dug graves and mopped brows with fervor."

"It's true. I worked nearly as hard as you." Hieronymus laughed with a raspy cough. There was no mirth in his expression.

Martin and Hieronymus turned the corner into the doorway of their dorm room only to be hit by a wall of stench. Two of their friends lay half naked on the ground, their chests and stomachs covered in angry red spots. "Typhoid fever," gasped Martin.

"Help us," groaned Günter.

"I cannot help you, friend. I will get the doctor." Martin pulled Hieronymus from the doorway into the hall. "Do not enter—we can do nothing at all to help them. I will get the doctor as I promised, but you must run find a priest. We cannot allow our friends to die without the sacrament of the last rites. We don't know where their souls will rest if we don't prepare them for the death that is certainly coming for them."

Hieronymus coughed again, his arms wrapped around his stomach. The young man sunk to the floor and Martin noticed that his skin had taken on an unearthly pallor. They had been so busy digging graves that Martin had failed to notice the change in Hieronymus.

"Hieronymus, are you not well?" Martin frowned in concern.

"Martin, do you remember when I said I was stronger than the dragon prowling? That I could fight Satan back?"

Martin nodded slowly.

Hieronymus looked at Martin with tears in his eyes. "Martin, I was a fool. Pray for my soul."

"I cannot." Martin's heart felt as though it would rend. He wanted nothing more than to hold his friend and pray over him, to comfort him. He shook off his sentimental nature and worked to gather his wits. "I will find a priest. The sacrament of the last rites must come only from the clergy."

Martin abandoned his friend Hieronymus on the cold stone floor while he sought a priest to pray for his friend's soul as it slipped from this world. Later that week, Martin buried Hieronymus outside the walls of the city beside his two dorm mates.

Throughout the year of 1503, the terror in Martin's heart grew. Martin had seen the prowling dragon. He had witnessed the serpent crouch, and the devastation as the firedrake devoured every living thing in its path, leaving in its wake havoc and ruin like the shell of a burnt-out tree after a well-placed lightning strike.

The stench of death eventually drifted from Erfurt, and Martin returned to his studies. He proved to be a brilliant student, with a secure and comfortable future ahead of him. As a lawyer, Martin could hope to become the counselor of a bishop or a prince, with the promise of gifts from his patrons. From a position of prominence, Martin would be able to care for his parents, and find reasonable appointments for his brothers. Over time, Martin slowly forgot the pain of his near-death experience, and returned to focusing on his studies. Martin loved to win, and "The Philosopher" won his debates over and over again.

Soon after the beginning of the New Year in 1505, Martin was awarded his master's degree amidst citywide parades.

"Master Martin, congratulations! How does it feel, man?" asked the housemaster, slapping Martin on the back.

Martin smiled broadly. "How great was the pomp and glory when masters were graduated, and torches were borne before them, and honors were showered upon them. I hold that no other temporal joys equaled these!"[11]

The housemaster laughed. "No worldly joys compare! You are correct, my good man. Take time to celebrate; your doctoral studies do not begin until May."

— ∎ —

In May 1505, twenty-two-year-old Martin entered law school. He studied under Jodocus Trutvetter, rector of the university, and Bartholomaus Arnoldi. Trutvetter had a great love of literature and poetry, and was not a fan of arguments over small issues. Rather, he liked to focus on the big picture. From Arnoldi, Martin learned to respect the Bible as a source of truth and to judge Scripture by the rest of Scripture. The Bible was to be studied in its entirety.

At the University of Erfurt, Martin learned many things that stood contrary to those he had studied as a child. He was taught that thunderstorms on a round earth came from wind and weather, not from dragons and witches. He found that the stars were not gods of the future, but lights in the sky. Martin's studies revealed that the Bible held its own in a battle against ancient writers and archaic knowledge. Yet, in the midst of his book learning, of the newest discoveries in science and literature, Martin was still a boy from the woods, who looked for the firedrakes of thunder in the sky.

It was during this time of discovery that Martin decided to go home to visit his parents. In May of 1505, he set out for a ten-day trip to see Hans and Margaretha Luther, became engaged, and started the fifty-mile trek back to Erfurt. His trip home was to change his life forever. Martin's thunderstorm—and his encounter with a stray lightning bolt—altered not only the path of his own life, but it was also to irrevocably blow the course of history onto a new path altogether.

Chapter 6

A TICKET TO HEAVEN

1505-1507

Saint Anna, help me." Martin screamed again, "I will become a monk!"

Covering his face with his arms, Martin rolled over in the mud beneath the burning elm, sobbing. As fiery branches began to drop near him like tongues of flame, the pitiful student recovered his wits and crawled through the rain to the side of the road, dragging his law books with him. He collapsed in the rocky mud, lying still and wailing until long after the rain had ceased.

When it became clear that his life had been spared, Martin climbed to his feet and limped toward Stotternheim, squinting his sore eyes in an effort to see. He knew the dragon had made a valiant attempt at vanquishing him. Martin had been stalked like a deer in an open field and he had been struck down. But Saint Anna had saved him. Martin had promised the saint of all miners his very life, and he would keep his promise.

Two weeks later, on July 17, 1505, twenty-one-year-old Martin stood before the imposing stone gates of the Augustinian monastery on the border of Erfurt's city center. Beside him, his friends gazed in awe at the massive double arches lining the walkway.

"It's not too late to change your mind, Martin."

"Martin, you still have a brilliant career as a lawyer ahead of you."

"Think of your mother and father, Martin. How will they make their way in the world, with no one to support them in their old age?"

Martin turned to his friends, sweat dripping from his brow, and steeled his heart. Clearly, his friends felt he was in grave error. Martin himself was not convinced that he truly desired to become a monk. Yet twice his cries for help in the face of certain death had been answered, and Martin had a debt to pay.

"It was good of you to come with me. I will take my leave now." Martin whispered a furtive prayer to Saint Anna and walked quietly into the long nave. Far ahead, past the space meant to allow for three hundred people to stand in worship, a high altar rose from the ground. A thin man dressed in a hairy black robe hunched on his hands and knees. With one hand, he scrubbed the stone floor with a coarse brush; with the other, he dragged a heavy metal bucket filled with water. The man's face was turned to the ground, and Martin could see his shaved scalp glimmering with bubbled reflections from his pail. Outside, the air had been warm and fragrant. Inside the nave, it was cool and smelled of dank stone.

The gaunt man looked up at Martin, a bushy ring of auburn hair circling his bare scalp. He did not sit up or rise, but peered at Martin from his hands and knees. Martin felt suddenly uncomfortable in his scholar's robe, clutching the two books of philosophy he had been unwilling to part with. His law books had already been sold. "What do you need?"

"I am here to become a monk."

"We do not need educated monks like you."

Martin hesitated. "Nonetheless, I promised Saint Anna, and I will keep my promise."

The monk sized up Martin before responding. "Well, I will not argue with Saint Anna. Go through the passage to your right. You will find a courtyard with the way of the cross. To the left, past the way of the cross, will be the common rooms. The brothers are eating a meal, and there you will find the prior."

Martin nodded. "Thank you."

He found the prior just as the monk said—through the door on the right, past the way of the cross in the courtyard, in one of the common rooms to the left. The brothers were all eating and the silence was nearly deafening. Martin ventured forward out of the muggy heat of the courtyard. He could nearly feel the breath of the angry dragon on his neck, daring him to step away from the promise he had made to pursue the easy life of a rich lawyer, yet every muscle in his body begged him to run in the opposite direction. Martin was not certain he could bear this mirthless, sober life. "I will not go to hell!" said Martin aloud. At once, twenty shaved heads turned in his direction, eyeing him with suspicion. The prior rose and narrowed his eyes.

"What is the meaning of this?" he asked.

Martin knelt before the prior with his head down. "I have come to be a monk."

"But you wear the robe of a scholar."

"I would give it up to follow God," said Martin nervously.

The prior nodded slowly. "Then you shall stay with us for a month. If you are still determined to become a member of the Observant Augustinians after thirty days, we will allow you to join us. Is that understood?"

Martin kept his eyes on the stone floor and nodded.

Time passed quickly. Martin had many conversations with the prior, discussing and analyzing his reasons for becoming a monk. Together, they poked and prodded the darker corners of Martin's soul.

On the morning of the thirtieth day, Martin rose at two o'clock in the morning from his straw bed, made the sign of the cross against his head and chest, and glanced about his small cell. There was a single table with a low chair, an open stone window, and a door. Martin had not even enough room to pace properly. At the second bell, he gathered his scholar's robes and walked the long hallway of the Augustinian Black Cloister.

Arriving at the nave, Martin dipped his fingertips in holy water and sprinkled himself before kneeling at the altar and praying a promise to devote himself in service to God. On either side of Martin and behind him, monks in black habits with shaved heads bowed in prayer as well.

For forty-five minutes, Martin sang songs in Latin to God—*Ave Maria,* the *Pater Noster,* and *Salve Regina* solemnly filled the air like a cloud of light pushing back the dark. Most mornings, Martin joined the monks as they exited the nave in pairs. This morning, however, he walked silently to the steps of the altar, where the prior stood frowning upon him.

Martin lowered himself to the cold stone floor. He pressed his forehead to the ground, his legs stretched behind him and his arms out to each side. He could hear the quiet rhythmic breathing of the monks behind him. His bare hands and feet grew cold as he waited.

"What do you seek, Martin?" asked the prior sternly.

"I seek God's grace, and His mercy."[1]

The prior took Martin by the elbow and pulled. Martin scrambled to his feet.

"Are you married, a slave, or diseased?"

"No," Martin replied with his eyes on the floor.

"Take your vows, then, of poverty, chastity, and obedience."

Martin thought his voice trembled some as he replied, "I, Brother Martin, make profession and promise obedience to Almighty God, to the Holy Virgin Mary, to the Holy Father Augustine, and to thee the prior of this convent, who stands in the place of the General of the Order, to live until death in poverty and chastity, according to the rule of Father Augustine."[2]

Behind Martin, the monks began a chant in honor of Saint Augustine. The fledgling monk's new brothers droned on as the crown of his head was shaved. One of the monks brought a small pile of clothing and set it in front of him. Martin removed his prestigious scholar's robe, replacing it with a white hair dress and a sleeveless black cloak over the top. There was a small black skullcap to cover the newly shaved portion of his head.

Martin laid on the floor once more, his arms stretched to his side in the shape of a cross while he breathed deep the dank wetness of the stone floor. He was certain the dragon would now leave him. Now he would see heaven.

The year of Martin's trial period seemed to move by quickly. Each morning he awakened at 2:00 AM to the sound of the cloister bell, and the day continued with a dizzying schedule of rituals. There was choir, confession, prayer, meditation, and exercise—Martin and a partner would walk silently up and down the cloister. The weather blew past the window in his small cell, and Martin shivered throughout the night, confident that his efforts would be noticed by a good and just God.

Martin exchanged letters with his father, Hans. Hans was furious over Martin's rash decision to join the Augustinian order and he refused to forgive his son. Then, in the late fall of 1505, Hans sent Martin a letter blessing his decision. Martin rejoiced over Hans's newfound acceptance, but mourned the news of the death of two of his brothers during another wave of the plague in his hometown, which swayed the hardened heart of his copper-mining father.

Even in the midst of the droning ritual of the monastic life, the brilliance of the former law student did not go unnoticed. Martin's superiors sent him to school to study to become a priest. He threw himself into his new role, learning all he could by day, and lying on the cold floor of his cell by night. Martin was determined to earn his way to God, whether it be through study and achievement or through self-denial and pain.

By 1507, nearly two years after he had joined the monastery, Martin was ready to say his first Mass as a newly ordained priest. He sent an invitation to Hans. Martin also summoned his old friends Vicar Braun and the Schalbes. For good measure, he also requested the presence of the monks of the Augustinian monastery that sat beneath the hulking Wartburg Castle, just outside of Eisenach.

It was a chilly morning in April when Martin walked the long hallway from his cell to the closet for his confession. Martin knelt before his confessor and superior, Johann von Staupitz, with his head down. "Forgive me, Father, for I have sinned. I have held bitterness in my heart toward my father; I have craved an extra piece of bread. I slept one night upon my straw bed, for my bones hurt, and the floor seemed far too unforgiving a foe." Martin continued until he had listed every sin he could recall or invent. Finally, relieved of his moral burdens, he was clean and ready to stand before the God of Heaven and Earth to offer the Lord's Supper.

With great expectation, Martin stood behind the altar. Before him in the nave were many of the men of Erfurt, as well as some of the guests he had invited from Eisenach.

He nodded to the crowd as he searched the faces for that of his father. Seeing that Hans was not there, Martin shored up his emotions and set himself to the task of directing the Mass. The familiar scent of incense filled his nostrils as he moved about the altar.

Without warning, the thunderous sound of galloping hooves against the cobblestones outside the nave resounded through the monastery. Hans Luther and twenty of his most important men strode down the aisle with confidence. Hans was dressed in a brightly colored tunic, with gold and copper jewelry upon his fingers and around his neck. His leggings made a brushing noise as he strode to the front of the nave, dropped one knee before the altar and crossed himself. Without smiling, he fixed his eyes on Martin from the front of the nave and waited.

Martin took hold of the loaf of bread and lifted it toward heaven. Little beads of sweat broke out upon his brow. *Who am I, that I should address the great Majesty, when all others tremble to appear in the presence of a prince or a king, or to address them?*[3] he thought in a panic. The new priest could feel Dr. Johann von Staupitz, the rector, eyeing him from the left, and Hans's gaze on him from the right.

"This is my body," said Martin, trembling. As he broke the loaf, his shaking hands faltered. The loaf—the body of Christ—pitched forward. Martin made a quick grab for the bread as the congregation gasped. His eyes were wet and blurred with sweat. *Who am I?* he thought again. *The angels surround Christ. At his nod the earth trembles. Shall I—a miserable little pygmy—say "I want this, I ask for that?" For I am*

dust and ashes and full of sin and I am speaking to the living
eternal and true God![4]

Martin felt the room spin. His stomach heaved, and
rivulets of sweat dripped from his chin. Lifting the chalice
of wine, he whispered, "This is the new testament of my
blood." His moist hands slipped and the cup fell backward.
Martin gasped and fought to hold the goblet upright. Over
the rim, he could see the disgusted expression of his father.

Chapter 7

THE STINKING SAND DUNE OF THURINGIA

1507–1510

Martin recovered his grip on the wine chalice and stumbled through the rest of the Lord's Supper in misery. His father, Hans, stood at the front of the line, glaring up at his son as he knelt to drink from the cup.

After Mass there was a feast to celebrate the new priest. Martin was finally able to speak to Hans across the trestle table in one of the common rooms. It had been nearly two years since the young priest had last seen his father, and he was confused by the older man's anger over his decision to commit to the monastery. After all, there was no greater spiritual calling than that of a monk.

"Dear father," Martin cleared his throat quietly. "Why have you opposed so greatly my service to God?" He paused, feeling much like the young boy who had fled from discipline, and offered his last defense. "God, glorious and holy in all his works, has deigned to exalt me, wretched and unworthy sinner, and to call me into his sublime ministry only for mercy's sake."[1] Surely no one could argue with the path of a serene man seeking God.

Hans spat. "Have you never heard that a man should honor his parents? Your position as a lawyer was to care for your mother and me."

Martin was nearly dumbstruck. "But, Father, I ought to be thankful for the glory of such divine goodness—as much as dust may be, for I am but dust—and to fulfill the duty laid upon me.[2] In this state I can be of more service to you, by prayer and other devotions, than if I had chosen some secular calling.[3] I was called here from heaven—by a voice from the thundercloud. I promised Saint Anna, Father."

Hans scowled. "You best hope along with me that it was not an apparition of the devil you saw!"[4] Rising from his seat, the successful copper-mine owner looked disdainfully around the common room, his eyes coming to rest upon his son with his coarse hair robe and skullcap. Hans summoned his men and the ensemble left the hall, their plates of food untouched.

— ∎ —

That year, between the spring of 1507 and the winter of 1508, Martin worked harder and harder for his salvation. He refused food and concentrated on listing his sins during confession before the prior over and over again. As a monk, it was difficult to get into any serious trouble, but Martin was certain that if he could only list every moment he felt anger, hunger, envy, or some equally devious transgression, he could perhaps be saved from the depths of hell.

"Martin." The prior walked purposefully toward the thin man who yet again had refused his supper. "I have something for you. It seems you have asked for a Bible."

"Yes." Martin did not dare to hope. He remembered wistfully the hours spent in the Magdeburg library where he first encountered the story of Samuel and Hannah. Oh, how he had wished for a Bible of his own—one not chained to a table, but free for him to carry about his daily tasks.

The corner of the prior's lip twitched as he drew a red leather tome from behind his back. "It is for you. You are to begin your studies in theology, now. You will work with one of the senior brothers to learn of those great theologians that have gone before us."

Aha, take that, O Dragon! Martin was triumphant. *It cannot be easy to hunt one who knows the Scriptures!*

As the months passed, Martin pored over his Bible. It was not the primary source of his studies in theology; rather, he was asked to read theologians like Peter Lombard, William of Occam, and Gabriel Biel. But in his free time, Martin read for hours in the pages of his most treasured possession.

Martin learned brilliantly. The skills he practiced as a law student had served him well in his studies at the monastery, and then at the nearby University of Erfurt as he became one of the few monks chosen to continue studying theology. As time wore on, Martin donned the look of a haunted man. His monkish dress hung from his bony frame and dark circles formed under his eyes and around his mouth. Martin's superiors could not help noticing the young man's intelligence—and his misery.

Dr. Johann von Staupitz visited the Erfurt cloister from time to time, one of the many monasteries he oversaw, and he had a special interest in meeting with the clever young monk. Martin was called from his studies and came blinking into the overcast gloom of the courtyard. He knelt before Dr. Staupitz, the rector of the German Augustinian Order, and bowed his head.

"You are very thin, Martin," said Dr. Staupitz gently.

"I find it best to fast, Father."

"I hear other things as well, my son. That you beat yourself, and deny yourself sleep. I have even heard that you sometimes lie on the floor all night long, spread out as a cross, after whipping yourself." The learned doctor frowned.

Martin's cheeks colored slightly. "It is not too much trouble to go to for my Lord. I work to become perfect, that God might accept my life after I die. I hope to confess to you my sins, Doctor Staupitz. Will you hear them?"

"Martin, you confessed to another just an hour ago."

"And I would choose to confess again." The wind blew against Martin's face. "I have felt anger toward my brother."

Staupitz shook his head. "You make yourself ill. God does not require your perfection, Martin. He requires only that you love him."

Martin glanced quickly at the doctor. Seeing that Staupitz was indeed serious, Martin stammered, "But Father—how can I love a God who is angry with me?"

"God is not angry with you, Martin. It is you who are angry with Him!"[5] The older man sighed and wrung his hands. "You're trying to find sins in yourself instead of trusting that God loved you first. He proved it by sending Jesus to die for your sins!"

Martin frowned. He did not wish to contradict his superior, but he was quite certain that God neither loved him nor cared for his soul. He believed the Lord to be a God of wrath and judgment without mercy. Martin left his conversation with Dr. Staupitz frustrated. Of course he was angry with God. How could a man not hate a God who required so much, yet promised no salvation in return? In the distance, a thunderclap reminded Martin that the dragon was ever stalking his very soul. He shivered at the thought of purgatory—that place where he was bound to pay for his sins once he died—and returned to his cell to beat himself once again, forgoing sleep, food, and warmth.

▬ ▬ ▬

Twenty-seven-year-old Martin stood in the brown, soggy grass overlooking a broad river in the winter of 1508. The bridge across the water rose to the top of a high embankment, crossing a stretch of land, then a stagnant moat, ending at the gate in the middle of a substantial stone wall that stretched for nearly a mile on its southern side. The monk wrinkled his nose as he took in the sight. The city was substantially smaller than Erfurt, and it squatted in the gentle curve of the River Elbe like a hapless toad. To his right the moat slopped into the river in waves, spilling stinking city drainage into the running water. Shimmering white sand bordered the reeking channel on either side, punctuated here and there by scrub brush.

A cold winter wind blew menacing clouds over the top of the city from the east. Martin shivered, then nearly gagged as the scent of human waste filled his nostrils. In a moment, his eyes widened as the sharp smell of rotting blood hit him. "Stockyards." Martin spat on the ground in disgust. "So this is the gem of Thuringia. It is a stinking sand dune, just as they say."

Martin continued his walk toward the bridge as he worked out a little tune in his head. He missed his lyre, but it did not stop him from singing in his quiet moments.

Little land, little land,
You are but a heap of sand.
If I dig you, the soil is light;
If I reap you the yield is slight.[6]

The priest grimaced and began his mile-long walk across the bridge to the city of Wittenberg, where he was to teach for the next year. "Staupitz, you old mule," he growled. "You have sent me close to the lair of the dragon itself. At least, it must be so, judging by the smell alone." Taking a deep breath of rancid air, Martin squared his shoulders and marched forward.

"State your business," came the gruff voice of a knight at the front gate.

"I have come under the order of my rector, Dr. Johann von Staupitz, to teach a year at the University of Wittenberg. I will be under the authority of the elector of Saxony,

Prince Frederick the Wise." Martin's eyes shifted from the knight to the dingy city before him.

"Carry on then, Professor."

On Martin's left, just through the massive gate, rose an impressive house with a tower that stretched the length of the block. Martin gazed up at it as he neared the end of the street and turned right. Staupitz had directed him to the far east side of the town, where the university buildings intermingled with houses. The houses ranged from grand mansions such as the one by the gate to small mud shacks with straw roofs. As Martin walked, the smell of the stockyard over the east wall grew stronger. At the far side of the town, the monk found a rectangular building, and beyond that, the newly erected frame of an Augustinian cloister. He investigated the grounds, entered the partially constructed building, and retreated to a large pear tree in the yard of the cloister.

"So." Martin sat on the cold ground and leaned his back against the tree. "I see they finished the sleeping quarters at least."

It didn't matter much to Martin. He was likely to sleep in the snow.

━━ ▪▪ ━━

Martin spent a year teaching in Wittenberg at Prince Frederick the Wise's new university before returning home to his bustling city of Erfurt in the autumn of 1509. There, he began giving theological lectures to monks in the cloister. Martin continued his studies of the Bible. He remained the serious, fearful monk, always seeking a way that he could earn less time in purgatory. Eating, sleeping, and warmth were luxuries Martin could not afford—not if he wished to flee the dragon forever, and to escape the judgment of an angry God.

In the winter of 1510, a quarrel arose among the Augustinian cloisters, and not even Doctor Staupitz could solve the issue in a friendly manner. He traveled to Erfurt and summoned Martin.

"Martin, you are aware of the disagreement?"

"Yes, I have been informed."

"We need a representative in Rome, the eternal city, and I have decided to send Johann von Mecheln."

Martin waited in silence. Johann was a wise choice as a delegate. He was Martin's senior, and he would represent the order well. Martin wondered why he had been summoned. Was he to help with the chores in Mecheln's absence? The tired monk could not possibly imagine shouldering any more responsibility. He felt a pang of envy as he realized that Mecheln would be traveling to the Holy City. *Oh, to be allowed to travel to Rome, where thousands of years can be lifted from the time in purgatory of one's relatives. The city where the Holy Father dwells.*

"Father, I have sinned," began Martin. Jealousy was a terrible sin, and Martin could not let it go unconfessed.

Staupitz shifted impatiently. "Martin. Johann will need a companion, and you shall accompany him. Ready yourself, you leave for Rome in the morning."

Chapter 8

O, HOLY CITY

1510–1511

Martin's gaze flew across the marble walls. Never in his life had he seen such extravagance. On every wall, magnificent works of art were painted in fresco. The emaciated monk suddenly felt as though he might retch. The room spun and he blinked hard to stop the floor from moving beneath him.

"Martin." Johann von Mecheln stood in the hallway with the Italian prior of the Santa Maria dell' Incoronata Monastery, waiting for his travel companion.

Martin's feet dragged leaden as he trudged after Mecheln. The pair had traveled silently, single file from Nuremberg, where Martin and Mecheln had met with a council, on through Germany and Switzerland. They began their journey in the bitter month of November. The snow started falling in Augsburg and continued as they struggled over the Alps. Now the pair had finally arrived in Milan, and the two men crumpled onto the straw mats offered to them in a small cell.

"That was nothing but an endless land of mountains and valleys." Martin closed his eyes with a weary groan.

"The Swiss are a surprisingly stalwart people," commented Mecheln.

Martin laughed dryly. "I am afraid the same cannot be said of me." He pressed on his stomach in an effort to settle the rolling waves of nausea. "Johann, I have not seen a monastery such as this. The cost of the paintings alone could feed every monk in Germany. Are these monks not sincere about their salvation? Did they not take a vow of poverty as we did?"

Mecheln's only answer was the subtle rumble of his throat as he slept.

Martin woke to a wincing pain as bells tolled for morning prayers. He struggled to open his eyes in the darkened room.

"Martin, you did not shutter the window last night." Mecheln's voice crawled forth as an irritated croak.

Martin struggled to swallow. His throat felt as swollen as his eyelids. Groaning, he lay on his mat and coughed. Outside the cell door, Martin could hear the steady footsteps of silent monks. There was a heavy knock, and the door swung open.

"They do not have morning Matins in Germany?" asked a surly voice.

Mecheln groaned. "My tongue is swollen, and my head aches."

The Italian monk closed a wooden barrier over the window and rolled the two Germans out of bed. "We observe Matins here, and I will see you attend." His Latin was heavily accented and Martin had to strain to make out the words.

Martin stumbled his way to the nave. The marbled halls glowed in the oil-lamp light, and he longed for the dead weight of the plain rock walls in the monastery at home. His head ached, and his tongue felt as though it had been replaced with a thick roll of linen in the middle of the night. Mecheln and Martin intoned a hymn and prayers, their ears ringing. After singing, the men retrieved their walking sticks and began again on their way through Milan.

"I need water, Martin." Mecheln paused by a trough outside a tavern. He placed his hands on the wooden rim and leaned over the cold liquid.

Martin shoved a horse aside and grabbed the shoulder of his companion. "That will be the death of you. You know as well as I do that typhoid comes from water." Martin's mind wandered back to his college friends—and to the graves he'd dug for them.

"I cannot drink wine, Martin. The thought is repulsive." Desperation laced Mecheln's voice.

"I cannot stomach it either, and yet I thirst terribly. I cannot continue our walk." The monks returned to the opulent monastery where they were ushered into hospice care.

"I can do nothing for you but recommend that you each eat a pomegranate," came the diagnosis. The miserable monks took the fruit and stumbled back to the cell reserved for visitors.

Early the next morning, Mecheln and Martin woke with cleared heads and an overwhelming thirst. They attended prayers, ate a cold breakfast, and proceeded on their way to Rome, healed by the strange fruit of membrane-wrapped pulp and seeds.

In silence, Martin trudged behind Mecheln through the lands of the Lombardy and the Po. *The fields here bring forth grapes and figs like nothing I have seen in Germany,* he thought. On the Po River they stayed at a Benedictine monastery with a massive yearly income. The food, drink, and lodgings were beyond anything Martin had imagined possible from his life in the little Thuringian cities. Even wealthy Erfurt began to look dingy and dirty from this side of the Alps. *Why would men sworn to the service of God engage in such decadence and display such a lack of self-control?* The alarming thought struck Martin like the broad edge of a sword.

The men left the Po, bent on covering at least twenty-five miles, as they had each day so far, with the exception of the extra night in Milan. The December sky was dark and threatening and Martin was anxious to reach Rome.

Florence was truly a site to behold, clean with magnificent buildings. Spectacular works of art were revealed at every turn. Martin marveled at the polite and bustling Italians. The men spoke with their whole bodies and wore tight clothing to show off their physiques. In the cities, the women wore veils; their jealous husbands insisted that no other man could see their face. Martin and Mecheln were able to tour several churches and hospitals, each time observing well-run institutions. Martin grew increasingly uncomfortable with the luxury and casual religion. He feared his old enemy might be waiting just around the next corner, a mass of scales and fire. In fact, he was not certain that the luxurious monasteries were not truly lairs for his nemesis.

At dinner the night the German monks slept in the Convent of San Gallo in Florence, an Italian monk waved his chicken leg in the air with a flourish. "Martíne, have you never heard of the monk Savonarola in that little forested town of yours?"

Martin eyed the excited man. "No. I have not."

The monk leaned forward. "Thirteen years ago, the fool Dominican held a bonfire of the vanities—calling people to repent, and burning thousands of paintings, books, and luxury items. Always talking about corruption in the monasteries, and helping the poor!" He speared the air with the drumstick. "The pope summoned the fool, and he would not come!"

A roar of laughter went through the hall.

Martin felt his temperature rise. "Are we not to help the poor and to avoid sinning with luxury?"

The hall grew quiet as death. Every eye was on Martin.

Finally, the monk across the table tore a chunk off his chicken, chewing slowly. He gulped before whirling the bone in the air above his head. "They tortured the man, and hung him! Then set fire to him so there was not one bone to bury!" Once again, the commons room roared with laughter, and the monks celebrated the victory of the church over the pitiful Savonarola by waving imaginary torches at each other.

For Martin, dinner was over. He excused himself and plodded to his cell, contemplating a pope who could condemn a man campaigning to rid the world of sin. Martin's legs screamed with the effort of marching nearly 850 miles in close to forty days. A fitful sleep overtook him, dreams of fire and Rome, of purgatory and freedom filling his night.

It was late December in 1510 when Martin and Mecheln reached Cassia Road and spotted the buildings of Rome rising above the landscape. Martin's misgivings disappeared. "Hail, holy Rome!"[1] he cried, throwing himself to the ground. "Three times holy because of the blood of the martyrs which flowed in thee, O, holy Rome!"[2]

By the time Mecheln and Martin arrived at the Santa Maria del Popolo monastery it was early January. Their first morning in the Holy City, the rain beat down on the two sodden monks as they trudged through the streets to bring their concern before the procurator of the Augustinian order. The official informed the monks that he would have his answer for them in a month.

"What will we do in Rome for four weeks?" Mecheln nudged a stone down a neglected street as the monks picked their way over fallen boulders from various Roman buildings.

"Tomorrow, we will see the relics of the saints!" Martin was brimming with plans for reducing the time his dead grandparents would spend in purgatory. The sun was just beginning to set as he stumbled across a fallen pillar. Human excrement lined the streets, and the remains of old Roman aqueducts ran over the city. Monks and nuns meandered past, telling coarse jokes and laughing at the tourists. Martin followed Mecheln's gaze to a procession walking past. A veiled woman dressed in ostentatious robes hurried across an open square with several armed guards in tow.

"Looks like she is concerned about something, doesn't it?" Mecheln glanced about the streets.

A small band of police approached the monks. "We must ask you to seek shelter for the night. If you return to the streets this evening, you will be imprisoned—if we reach you first."

"Who else would reach us?" Martin wondered aloud.

The Italian law keepers looked at each other and laughed uproariously. "Well, you will find out if you remain outside. There are only three hundred of us policemen— not enough to guarantee your safety."

Rattled, Martin and Mecheln quickened their pace.

That evening, the monks in the common room at Santa Maria del Popolo held discussions much like those of the monks in Florence. There was laughing and drinking, and several monks spat out God's name like a bone from their chicken. Martin was appalled. *Where is the holiness in this holy city?*

Martin raised his voice above the din. "We should like to make our pilgrimage to the churches tomorrow. Can that be arranged?"

The monks eyed Martin before one volunteered. "I can take you. Perhaps you would like to see the paintings of the master Raphael? He is painting frescoes upon the walls of the Stanza della Signatura. There is another artist—Michelangelo, I think is his name—he is to paint the new ceiling of the chapel in St. Peter's church, but the dome is still being constructed. The artist says he is only a sculptor, but the Holy Father has worn him down, and he has agreed to paint the ceiling. If there is anything Pope Julius II loves, it is art. Well, art—and war."

Martin's eyes grew wide. "The pope loves war?"

The monks roared with laughter. "The Soldier Pope is at war even as we speak!"

"He rides at the front of the troops!"

"This very night, he is fighting through snow in France to take Mirandola."

"Soon, Rome should rule the world!"

Martin spent a sleepless night, trying to process all he had learned that day. Rome was violent, dirty, and broken down. Worse, the pope was a warrior with a love for expensive artwork. One of the monks had even said the pope had three daughters! *Impossible*, thought Martin. *It must be a lie, for he took a vow of celibacy. I shall see the relics of the saints tomorrow in this eternal city, and rejoice in their holiness. Certainly, I will not be drawn in by worldly artwork.* When the distraught monk finally napped just before dawn, he dreamt of dragons prowling the streets of Rome in the moonlight.

"Keep up!" The Italian monk nearly ran through the streets of Rome toward the San Paolo gate.

"What is that building?" puffed Martin, rivulets of rainwater running through his hair and down his chin. "The one with all of the archways?"

The monk led Martin and Mecheln to an entrance in the wall of a massive structure. Inside the partially crumbled enclosure, tiers of seating rose skyward while a stone maze sat on the ground at the center. "There used to be a wooden floor there." The monk pointed. "The maze is where the gladiators, lions, bears, and Christian saints were kept. Trap doors would open, and the crowds would see a Christian and a lion emerge together." Martin stared aghast at the labyrinth below him. Looking up, he noticed stray cattle were eating sodden grass in the tiers of the ruins.

Again, their tour guide headed south. Martin and Johann struggled to keep up, climbing over debris from Rome's earlier days. They arrived gasping and wet at the Church of San Paolo. "The bodies of Peter and Paul are over there. Kiss the silver crosses above them and you will receive 17,000 years of indulgences. That's 17,000 years you don't have to suffer in purgatory." The monk gestured widely, clearly bored with this journey already. "Behind that wall lie buried the bodies of three hundred children from Bethlehem." He yawned. "The same children that were killed by evil King Herod when Jesus was just a baby."

Martin looked at the apathetic monk and whispered to Mecheln, "That we can borrow from the good deeds of the saints and thus have less punishment is a wonderful mystery!" He refused to let the Roman guide's cynicism affect his excitement.

As they toured San Paolo, the German monks were shown a column against which Saint Paul had preached while in Rome. This was what Martin had longed for, a pilgrimage to see the saints and the land of Saint Paul.

Here, he could pray over the relics and receive indulgences for less time in purgatory for loved ones. Martin nearly laughed with glee at the thought.

The day was long. The three monks trudged from one church to another, making a wide circle around Rome, then back through the center. Martin saw the Samaritan woman's grave, a stone with a footprint of Christ, an altar that contained a piece of rope that had been tied to Jesus as he was dragged toward his death, the sponge used to give Jesus a drink on the cross, and the catacombs in which early Christians hid from the Roman soldiers bent on their destruction. There was the sword that beheaded Paul and pieces of the burning bush before which Moses had stood. Martin prayed over countless pieces of bone, cloth, and gravesites, and donated coins at each station to help pay for the indulgences.

Each time he saw a small piece of bone, Martin tried to imagine it as one of the saints. He envisioned his prayers being received by Mary or Paul or Stephen and delivered to Christ. Martin tried to believe that his money given at each church was helping to peel years off of the sentences of relatives in purgatory. A gnawing uncertainty grew as he raced through the ruins of Rome to gaze upon another relic. *Will these bits of rope and cloth truly make a difference in eternity?*

A few of the churches Martin and Mecheln visited held Mass. The services were rushed, as if the priests had somewhere else to be. At one service, Martin stood to say Mass, barely able to contain his excitement. He closed his eyes and took a deep breath. The Italian monk overseeing the assembly looked up at Martin and growled, "Brother, move, move! Send her son home to our Lady speedily!"[3] Martin stumbled through the words, feeling as though a sword had passed through his heart. *This is the Eternal and Holy City?*

Near the end of their whirlwind day, Mecheln and Martin followed their guide to the Scala Santa. Martin paid close attention to the road, always looking for pieces of the broken Roman Empire in his path.

"The Scala Santa!" Martin's excitement returned. "I have dreamed of climbing all twenty-eight of these stairs as our Lord Jesus did on his way to Pontius Pilate's house, when he was sentenced to death!" Martin stood at the bottom of the stairs, wondering how the church had managed to move the heavy marble steps from Jerusalem all the way to Rome.

Brushing the thought aside, Martin knelt with great reverence upon the bottom stair and intoned the Lord's Prayer. Kissing the step, he crawled to the next stair on his knees and prayed again. Again he kissed the marble and again he prayed. At the top, Martin knew that the soul of a relative would be released from purgatory. Martin crawled to another step. His back ached and slivers of pain ran from the unforgiving rock through his knees and up his legs. He began to say the Lord's Prayer yet again when a thought ran through his mind.

The just shall live by faith.

Martin stared at the worn, dirty marble in front of him. "Our Lord . . ." he began. The thought came again.

The just shall live by faith.

Martin considered his journey through Italy: the magnificent monasteries, beautiful artwork, the Soldier Pope, and the bits of bone and cloth. He shook his head, finished his prayer, and kissed the stair beneath him. Martin labored to the top step, prayed, kissed the stair, and struggled to his feet.

Martin stood atop the Scala Santa stairs and gazed upon Rome. All around him stood the ruins of the past, palaces of the cardinals, over seventy monasteries, and cows grazing in the Colosseum. With horror, he realized that this city, this Eternal and Holy City, might just be the lair of the dragon he had spent his life fleeing.

Martin put both hands to his face. With a guttural cry of despair, he shouted: "Who knows whether this be true!"[4]

Chapter 9

TRUTH REIGNS

1511–1515

Martin sat in the summer sun beneath his favorite pear tree in the garden of the Black Cloister in Wittenberg with his red leather Bible open on his bony lap. For months now, he had been reading through Scripture with a mixture of fascination and repulsion. Finally, he had finished every book; it had been his first time all the way through the Word of God. When the twenty-seven-year-old monk saw his friend and superior, Doctor Staupitz, approaching from College Street, he closed the cover.

"Martin. Your Bible is shut."

"I have just finished reading it all the way through."

"And have you found what you are looking for?"

Martin sighed. "I am confused. I preach the message of the church in Rome—the pope's message—that if a man confesses each and every sin, and does his penance, he will be saved—saved to purgatory, where he will pay again for his sins. Yet, how does a man know that he has confessed every sin? How does he know that he has found every stray thought and repented?

"Despair is also a great concern to me. I teach, like the pope, that despair is the gravest of all sins. If I give in to depression, I will never see heaven." Martin closed his eyes. "I must confess that if I spend too long looking for my secret sins, I feel that I begin to despair. There is no way to be assured of my salvation."

Staupitz looked down upon his friend. "What of your idea that we all have a spark of goodness deep in our souls? That there is a remnant of good remaining in us, and we can work our way to God through this—warring against sin?"

Above the pear tree, a cloud rolled across the light of the sun, and the garden darkened. Martin shivered in his hair dress. Instinctively, his eyes scanned the fenced lot for a glint of scales or a column of nostril steam. "Yet, our love of self is the sum of all vices. How can a remnant spark of goodness be real? Have you read this book?" Martin shook his Bible at his rector. "The men within it are evil of heart. From the Fall, there has been no good within us."

Staupitz sat on the ground with a sigh. "And have you given much thought to what I have taught you? The way of the mystic is one of peace. If you just love God enough, He will love you back, and His Spirit will overwhelm your nature."

Martin stared at Staupitz. "I have tried this path, Doctor. I have attempted to love God, who is a just and holy judge, and not at all approachable. For days, I felt amazing, as though I were soaring among choirs of angels.[1] Yet, now I feel as though I have dropped into the abyss. I cannot locate this idea in Scripture, either.

"Do you not know that God dwells in light inaccessible? We weak and ignorant creatures want to probe and understand the incomprehensible majesty of the unfathomable light of the wonder of God. We approach; we prepare ourselves to approach." Martin bowed his head in frustration. He thought perhaps he could hear the faint rustle of wings and the clink of scales. "What wonder then that his majesty overpowers us and shatters!"[2]

There was a long silence as Staupitz considered this outburst. "And the way of the Augustinian—of our order? Saint Augustine taught that God has already decided our fate. In this case you should not worry." He smiled at the forlorn priest.

Martin erupted. "Is it not against all natural reason that God out of His mere whim deserts men, hardens them, condemns them, as if He delights in sins and in such torments of the wretched for eternity, He who is said to be of such mercy and goodness?"[3]

Martin shook his head. *How could a just God not allow a man to even know if he had been selected for salvation? How does this fit with Rome's teaching that I can work my way to heaven through my own merit?* "This appears iniquitous, cruel, and intolerable in God, by which very many have been offended in all ages. And who would not be?"[4]

Staupitz was calmly listening. Martin decided that this was the moment for his outburst to finish. If his words sent him to hell, then so be it. He could no longer keep his painful thoughts contained. "I have been driven to the very abyss of despair! I wish I had never been created. Love God? I hate Him!"[5]

A wind swept through the upper leaves of the pear tree. Martin was certain the dragon was circling above him like a vulture, smelling his very blood running from his soul. He was certain that he had just blasphemed the name of the one, true God. Martin could feel the invisible talons of his enemy tightening about him. He was guilty, and God could only condemn a man such as himself to the depths of hell. No matter how many hours Martin spent beating himself, he would never rise above his own sin.

Staupitz stared at Martin in disbelief. "I don't understand it! How can you say such a thing? I have never experienced trials such as yours, but I think they are more needful for you than your meat and drink!"[6] Staupitz appeared irritable. Martin realized that his superior had just given him several seemingly contradictory ideas. Could it be that Doctor Staupitz himself did not truly understand how humans could be saved? In a final burst of frustration, Staupitz raised his voice several levels. "Christ died for the forgiveness of your sins!"

Martin watched Staupitz roll his eyes and sigh heavily before storming in circles around the yard of the Black Cloister. The cloud above him had rolled away, and the sun warmed Martin's chest and face while the cold bark of his favorite pear tree pressed against the bones in his back.

Staupitz returned to glare down at Martin with an air of controlled authority. "You will focus on teaching others. You will earn the degree of a doctor, and become the head of theology at the University of Wittenberg. You will lecture for the students, and preach at the Castle Church for all of Wittenberg to hear."

Martin stumbled to his feet. "But—I am not strong. It will be the death of me!" It was far too much work for one sinful, mortal man, and Martin knew it.

Staupitz grimaced at his charge and slowed his speech, as though lecturing a toddler. "It seems that our God will soon have much to do in heaven and upon earth, therefore He will need many industrious doctors to perform the work. Whether you live or die, God will use your work."[7] With that, he turned and stalked off in the direction of College Street.

"No!" Martin called lamely after Staupitz. The vicar-general of the Augustinians showed no sign of hearing the priest.

Martin made no effort to obey his mentor, but Staupitz returned to see him just months later in September of 1511, demanding that Martin earn his doctorate of theology, and become the head of theology at the little university—a job for which Staupitz himself was responsible. In order to secure his own release from the job, Staupitz promised Prince Frederick the Wise that Martin would remain at the university for the remainder of the monk's life.

In 1512, Martin was elected the subprior of the Wittenberg monastery—a job that made him the second-in-command. That same year, he earned his doctorate of theology, becoming Dr. Martinus Lutherus, the proper Latin title for a man of his stature. He began to teach at the university, becoming the chair of the theology department. It was late in October of 1512 when Martin began to lecture on the book of Genesis at seven each morning. He was given a small office of his own in which to study and prepare. Martin was nothing if not prepared. He spent hours studying the Bible, working to understand the books on which he was assigned to preach. In August of 1513, Martin began to teach the Psalms to his students.

━━ ▪ ━━

Martin dipped his pen in the well of ink and returned to his paper. His little room in the southwest corner tower of the castle overlooked the Elbe River. A foul wind blew through the open window, choking him and bringing tears to his eyes. *I shall never grow accustomed to the smell of the stockyards!* Martin remembered the first time he had seen that river from the fields he overlooked. Now, in the summer of 1513, that seemed long ago. Concentrating, he returned to the letter he was writing to a friend:

> *I require two secretaries, for I do nothing almost all day but write letters, therefore if I repeat myself you will understand why it is. I am lecturer in the cloister, reader at meals, preach daily, and direct the students' studies, am the Prior's vicar (which means being vicar eleven times over), inspector of fish ponds at Litzkau; must espouse the Hertzberg people's cause at Torgau, expounder of Saint Paul and the Psalms, besides my letter-writing. Behold what a leisurely man I am.*[8]

Martin laughed wryly to himself. Even as an over-worked monk, the young man was still as sarcastic as he had been in his days as a law student at the University of Erfurt. He set the letter aside, pulling toward himself the thick copy of Psalms he had ordered to be printed with a single column on the page and wide margins for his notes. It was opened to Psalm 22, and he began to read aloud from the first verse:

My God, my God, why hast thou forsaken me?

Martin nearly choked on the words. He stood, pacing his small room. *What could these words mean?* he thought. *These are the words of Christ upon the cross. How could Jesus, the judge of all men, have questioned God? Was this not Christ's plan all along?*

Martin gasped and stood in the center of the room, stale air sticking in his throat. Little drops of sweat ran down his back as he stared out the window at the river beyond the city wall. Martin didn't see the river. Rather, he saw a man, beaten and bruised, hanging on a cross just before his death.

"I am forsaken," the priest whispered aloud. "My sin has made me abandoned by God. But Jesus—how could Jesus be forsaken when he was pure and without sin?" Martin gasped. "Jesus took my sin! He was separated from God for me and my wickedness! He bore my sin on the cross."

Martin realized that even his toes were sweating. Leaving his printed lecture copy on his table, he turned and climbed down the long, winding staircase of the tower. As Martin walked quietly from the castle into the garden, he paused, recognizing the voice of Dr. Polich von Mellerstadt, one of the founders of the university. "This monk will confuse all the doctors, introducing a new doctrine. He will reform the Roman church, for he devotes himself to the writings of the prophets and apostles, and takes his position upon the word of Jesus Christ, which no one is able to refute or overthrow with philosophy or sophistry."[9]

He heard another man murmur in agreement, and their footsteps as they walked through the garden gate onto Cleric Street. Martin shook his head in confusion. Was he not supposed to preach from Scripture—the very Word of God? He thought again of his encounter with the Bible minutes before. Martin would need a good night's sleep to understand his new findings. *Can it truly be that the words of Christ rank above those of councils and popes?*

For once, Martin slept on his straw mat, rather than on the wooden floor.

━ ∎ ━

Martin stared again at Psalm 71. He stood to pace, rubbing the top of his bald head with his hand. He found he thought better out loud. "Why would God deliver me and rescue me in His righteousness? It is this righteousness that I hate! It is His righteousness that separates me from Him! My works bring me no closer to salvation. All the whippings, the fasting, the sleeping outside—even in the snow! I am no closer to heaven or even to purgatory. Yet, this psalm tells me the Lord is my hope. How can this be?"

Outside Martin's window, the rain beat down merci-
lessly. The thunder and lightning churned against his raw
emotions and he closed his eyes, willing the memory of
his day beneath the tree outside Stotternheim to disappear.
He sank to his rough wooden chair and turned the pages
in his red leather Bible until he found the words of Paul. *I
will leave the Psalms for tonight. Perhaps this will be the night I
understand Paul.*

The priest turned to the first chapter of Paul's letter to
the Romans and began to read aloud. His eyes riveted to
the page when he reached verses 16 and 17.

*"For I am not ashamed of the gospel of Christ: for it is the
power of God unto salvation to everyone that believeth; to the
Jew first, and also to the Greek."* Martin considered this
verse for several minutes, listening to the rain pummel the
roof above him. This verse promised salvation to all who
believed. He continued reading, *"For therein is the righteousness of God revealed from faith to faith: as it is written, The just
shall live by faith."*

Martin jumped to his feet. These were the very words
he had thought as he climbed the marble steps of the Scala
Santa in Rome. But what did they mean? *I am neither just,
nor full of faith.*

The confused theologian paced the room, his thoughts
spinning recklessly against each other, jumbling every Bible
verse he had ever read and remembered against the others,
like men jousting and jostling for position. His head ached
with the pain of thinking.

"Could it be?" Martin stopped abruptly, staring down
at the Bible on the table in his small upper room. He drew a

deep breath. "The same God who judges the sinner—who requires faith to believe—gives the faith. The faith comes by hearing and studying the Word of God. It is an act of mercy that He gives the faith. It is by grace I am saved through the faith that He gives!"

Chapter 10

THE NEW THEOLOGY AND A NEW MAN

1515–October 1517

M artin, the subprior of the Augustinian order, the head of the theology department at Wittenberg University, and the priest of the Castle Church and the Town Church, was finally saved from his sins. He read Scripture with a new understanding of God's love, grace, and mercy. No longer did Martin see Jesus only as an angry judge, ready to throw men into hell. Martin knew Jesus as his Savior, God-made-man, who took the sins of every person upon Himself. The Savior died on a cross and rose again from the dead for the sins of Martin, and it was Martin whom Jesus had been pursuing.

Martin began to see the students and professors around him as equally pursued by God's love. More and more, his preaching was based on the Word of God. The change was so noticeable that others began to call his teaching the "New Theology."

News of the New Theology spread. The students of Wittenberg packed Martin's classes. Little by little, the wealthy men and women of the town began to attend the priest's lectures as well. Every man and woman of Wittenberg wanted to hear this new teaching of God's love—the teaching that came out of Dr. Luther's big red book. Among those attending Martin's lectures were three men who became important lifelong friends. Georg Spalatin, Johann Lang, and Nicholas von Amsdorf all came to know the love and grace of Jesus while sitting in the lecture hall at the University of Wittenberg. Johann Lang was a Greek scholar and Martin added the study of this language to his other responsibilities as he continued to analyze the Bible and lecture.

From November of 1515 to September of 1516, Martin taught classes on his beloved book of Romans. It was during that time that his sermons began to raise concerns among some of the spiritual and political leaders in his part of Germany.

"I have been to Rome." Martin grasped the edge of the podium and leaned toward the crowded galley of the small Castle Church. "On the way to and from the Holy City, many times have I looked upon the entire robe of our Lord, woven in one solid piece.[1] I must ask you to consider this: How many robes must have been owned by Christ?

Christ—Jesus, who as a fox without a hole, lacked a place to lay his head at night?"

Nervous laughter erupted from children. Throughout the church, wives looked to their husbands in confusion and men furrowed their brows. "Our good and kind prince, the elector of Saxony, himself has a collection of relics that rivals any I have seen. There is a piece of bread blessed by Christ himself during the Last Supper, four hairs from Our Lady, Christ's mother. There is from the crib a clipping of the swaddling clothes, a wisp of straw, and a piece of the gold brought by the Magi. You can locate four pieces of Saint Chrysostom, and six pieces of Saint Bernard. Why, there are more than 19,000 holy bones altogether! Were you to pray to every relic in the collection of Prince Frederick the Wise, you would reduce the time in purgatory of your loved one by one million, nine hundred two thousand, two hundred two years." Martin frowned deeply. "And two hundred seventy days."

At this, a boy in the front row laughed loudly. Martin waved his red leather Bible. "The Holy Scriptures describe man as so focused on himself that he uses physical and even spiritual goods for his own purposes. Man, I say, turns all these things to himself, seeks his own good in them all." Martin paused to let his point sink in. "Man horribly makes idols out of them in place of the true God. We make God into an idol and the truth of God into a lie!"[2]

There was a gasp throughout the congregation. Martin Luther, the teacher of the New Theology, had accused the people he discipled of idolatry. Like a knight in a great battle, Martin had thrown down the gauntlet and declared his intent. Martin intended to preach a life based on Scripture rather than on human tradition.

It was April 1516 when the prince of Saxony decided to examine the situation.

━━ ▪ ━━

"If you have a true faith that Christ is your Savior, then at once you have a gracious God." Martin allowed a few moments so his students could process this. "For faith leads you in and opens up God's heart and will, that you should see pure grace and overflowing love. This is to behold God in faith that you should look upon his fatherly, friendly heart, in which there is no anger nor ungraciousness. He who sees God as angry does not see him rightly."[3] Martin saw several confused faces in the hall. He remembered feeling equally confused by God's love just a few years ago under his favorite pear tree while talking to Doctor Staupitz.

In the back, Martin's friend Nicholas von Amsdorf leaned against a wall and nodded approvingly with a little smirk on his face. He motioned with his chin to two well-dressed men several rows down. Martin's eyes widened slightly. *So,* he thought, *Prince Frederick the Wise has sent his lawyers to examine the situation. I know that Georg Spalatin has begun to talk with the good prince in the hopes of convincing him to teach classes strictly from the Bible.*

Martin shook himself slightly and continued. "He who sees God as angry does not see him rightly but looks only on a curtain, as if a dark cloud had been drawn across his face."[4]

By summer, there had been no word of rebuke from the prince. Martin continued to preach with passion and newfound strength from God's Word.

— ■ —

It was a warm, sunny day in Thuringia when the people of Wittenberg began to die. Once again, the nightmare of the plague snaked into Martin's life.

"Martin. You must leave. We cannot afford to lose you. Your New Theology is drawing students to the school. You preach truth from God's Word. You must flee."

Martin shifted inside his hair tunic and grimaced. His mind returned to the days when he dug grave after grave, placing the bodies of his friends beneath the earth. He remembered his brothers who had died at the hand of the Black Death. Martin shuddered.

"How many do we lose?"

The reply was grim in a city so small. "Two to three die each day."

Martin considered the pain of the people of Wittenberg, knowing that within weeks the city could become a ghost town. Yet, the people needed a pastor. The Word of God must be preached, especially in times of great suffering. The priest steadied his voice. "I will stay. The world will not come to an end although Brother Martin perish. Not that I have no fear of death, but I still hope the Lord will deliver me from this fear also."[5] With that, it was settled. Martin Luther would stare into the eyes of the beast and trust in Jesus for his courage.

— ■ —

It was October 31, the night of All Hallow's Eve in 1516, when Martin preached against indulgences for the first time. The surviving townspeople of Wittenberg were weary from their bout with an invisible foe they did not understand. True to his word, Martin had remained to counsel the sick, doctor the dying, and preach to the survivors. Pope Leo X had worn the triple crown of the Roman church for three-and-a-half years when his lavish spending on feasts, pageants, and gambling crept into the purses of the German peasants.

Martin stormed through the dank halls of the Black Cloister. "They are to sell indulgences in Saxony! Indulgences!"

His blood boiled when he considered poor peasants scraping together their meager resources to buy a piece of paper relieving a dead family member of a certain number of years in purgatory. *Could the saints truly store merit in heaven? Could that merit be purchased by a human? Was that not similar to trying to earn salvation through works? Weren't the just saved by faith through the gift of grace?*

A nearby monk looked upon Martin's disheveled robe and scrawny body with a raised eyebrow. "It offends you that the peasants wish to avoid time in purgatory for those they love?"

Martin turned on the monk. Even his carefully clipped tonsure appeared wind blown. "Christ has nowhere commanded indulgences to be preached, but the gospel!"[6]

Martin left the bewildered monk and marched up College Street toward the Town Church. By the time he arrived, he felt he could hear once again the clank of weapons, the creak of armor, and the stirring of the great dragon. His nostrils filled with the dust and smoke of a monstrous fight. Tonight he would war against the flying worm. He would preach against the insidious, creeping lie that a piece of paper could save a man from his sins.

Chapter 11

THE BREAKING POINT

October 30–31, 1517

Martin strode along College Street on his way back to the Black Cloister following his last lecture for the afternoon, the crisp fall air grazing his naked scalp. In the morning it would be exactly one year since Martin had first preached against indulgences. In the last year, he had preached on the subject a total of three times. It seemed to Martin that the more he spoke about the indulgences, the stronger his feelings of disdain and disgust grew. Ahead, a large group of Martin's congregants moved toward him from the direction of the Elster Gate.

That's odd, thought Martin. *There are rich and poor, young and old—all walking together. Perhaps they are celebrating All Hallow's Eve in some new manner?*

"Doctor Luther!" A young boy ran forward waving a parchment scroll, clearly excited. Past the new college and the old, past houses lining the street, he ran toward Martin. Behind him trailed a group of boys and girls, all with the same ruddy features and tawny hair. "Look at my indulgence! Mother sent us to meet the pope's monk in Jüterbog to buy an indulgence for Father now that he is in purgatory."

"You walked all the way to Jüterbog?"

The boy's older sister nodded. She shivered beneath her threadbare dress. "We left two days ago and we slept in market square." In spite of her shivering, the girl's eyes lit up with the memory of her journey. "The town criers announced the coming of a monk—I think his name was Johann Tetzel—and then the trumpets started blowing."

A small crowd of children surrounded Martin, puffing from the run down the street to catch up with the siblings. "Doctor Luther, there were horsemen and drummers too!"

"And a big cross!" announced a small child. Martin frowned.

"There was a parade! A man dressed in fancy clothes carried a velvet pillow embroidered with gold, and on the pillow lay the pope's bull—the pope signed it himself!"

A sturdy youth joined the group. "There were many people walking with flags and candles, and a giant chest, and the church bells were sounding."

"Then came the monk Johann Tetzel. He had many guards."

"He preached on a wooden platform."

"I couldn't see!"

Martin rubbed his tonsure in quick, jerky movements. His head was beginning to hurt. He could imagine the scene now with peasants and noblemen alike crowding and jostling to get a chance to purchase the forgiveness for a loved one's sins, frantic for the opportunity to overcome years of torture in purgatory as payment for sins Christ's death had already justified on the cross. He turned to the boy. "Tell me, child, how much did you spend?"

"We spent a half a gulden."

"Yes," interrupted his sister again. "But some people spent much more. I saw one bishop pay twenty-five guldens."

Martin fixed his nearly black eyes on the girl. "A bishop? He purchased an indulgence for a family member for that price?"

The sturdy young man guffawed. "Nein, Doctor Luther, the bishop bought the indulgence for himself. This indulgence is not like the others we've seen sold—this indulgence forgives all sins completely for the buyer."

"What?" Martin grabbed the rolled parchment the young boy was clutching. Scanning the document, he began to mutter aloud. "We are saved by faith in Jesus Christ. We have faith only through grace—it is Jesus who saves."

As he handed the indulgence back to the boy, a wealthy businessman walked past and waved a paper in Martin's direction. "Doctor Luther! For six gulden, I have purchased my own salvation. You should not expect me in confession again." The man laughed. "For as long as I have this paper, I am free from guilt!"

Martin's head was spinning. He felt a sharp pain in his stomach as he called after the merchant. "Those souls which have believed this—that through indulgences a man is freed from all penalties—are being led in the paths of death!"[1]

"I have a paper signed by the pope that says otherwise, Doctor!" With that, the man turned onto Mayor Street and was gone. The children ran off singing, "Once a coin in the coffer rings, the soul from purgatory springs!" They repeated it until Martin could no longer hear them.

Martin stood in the road as peasants, merchants, and knights streamed past him, the wind spinning the dirt from the road into little whirlwinds. He strained to hear above the general din surrounding him. From the direction of Jüterbog, he was certain he could hear the fiery cackle of his old enemy the dragon.

— ■ —

Later that afternoon, Martin paced his tower office in the Black Cloister. The air in the little room was musty and chilled. Martin's irritation was so severe, he spoke aloud, aiming his words at God, the devil, or whoever else might be inclined to listen. "Pay for Saint Peter's Basilica on the back of the German peasantry! Why, if the pope knew about the poverty of the German people—if he saw the dress that barely warms the girl. . . . Pope Leo X is a good pope. He would rather have Saint Peter's church in ashes than have it built with the flesh and bones of his sheep![2] It is the sellers of indulgences who are cruel beyond all cruelty, not freeing souls for charity, though they do for money."[3]

Martin's eyes glistened in the candle-lit room like a jaguar on the prowl. No longer feeling hunted, Martin imagined himself the hunter. He was out for dragon blood tonight.

I must write it down, he thought. *If the pope can see the objections from Scripture, he will change. In fact, we will have a debate—I will invite all of the scholars from universities far and wide to discuss indulgences. I will need the printer, Johann Gruenenberg, to make copies so I can send a copy to Archbishop Albert of Brandenburg. He is a wise and holy man, and he will make this right—he cannot possibly know what is occurring in his own territory, or he would never allow it.*

"First," Martin said aloud and with renewed vigor now that he had a plan, "it is vain conceit to think that the pope could remove all penalties for sin. For, the only penalties he can remove are the ones he himself has imposed! How does he plan to exercise authority over purgatory except through prayer?"[4] Martin paused, impressed by the weight of his own logic. "Why does the pope not empty purgatory, for the sake of holy love and due to the dire need of the souls that reside there, if he redeems an infinite number of souls for the sake of miserable money with which to build a church? To free needy souls for the sake of love would be most just—to free them only for money is most trivial."[5] Martin was nearly shouting now. He boxed the air as though warming up for his joust with the enemy.

"What is more, indulgences cannot save from even the least of sins, much less absolve a man of the guilt of the most impossible of sins. Is teaching this not madness?"[6] Martin pulled out a long sheet of paper and a freshly sharpened goose quill, ready to record the list of objections forming in his brilliant mind. Then he had a thought that fired his anger to an even hotter fury.

"And finally, the true treasure of the church is the Most Holy Gospel of the glory and the grace of God. But, of course, this is the very treasure that is most hated, for it makes the first to be last. Yet the treasure of indulgences makes the last to be first and is loved."[7] Martin paused to think, his brow furrowed in concentration. "The treasures of the Gospel are nets with which the Church formerly fished for men of riches." His voice intensified as he stabbed his quill in the little ornate jar of ink. "And now! The treasures of indulgences are nets with which the Church fishes for the riches of men!"[8]

By now, the list was ready in Martin's mind. He sat before his desk and carefully wrote:

1. Our Lord and Master Jesus Christ, when He said, "Repent" (Matthew 4:17), willed that the whole life of believers should be of repentance.

Martin wrote point after point on his paper, carefully stating his case, just as he had learned during his training to be a lawyer.

6. The pope cannot remit any guilt, except by declaring that it has been remitted by God and by assenting to God's remission . . .
36. Every truly repentant Christian has a right to full remission of penalty and guilt, even without letters of pardon.

45. Christians are to be taught that he who sees a man in need, and passes him by, and gives his money for pardons, purchases not the indulgences of the pope, but the indignation of God.

54. Injury is done to the Word of God when, in the same sermon, an equal or a longer time is spent on pardons than on this Word.

86. Again: Why does not the pope, whose wealth is today greater than the riches of the richest, build just this one church of St. Peter with his own money, rather than with the money of poor believers?

94. Christians are to be exhorted that they be diligent in following Christ, their Head, through penalties, deaths, and hell;

95. And thus be confident of entering into heaven rather through many tribulations, than through the assurance of peace.[9]

Martin sighed deeply as he looked over his list of ninety-five theses written in Latin so that only other scholars and church officials could understand them. Satisfied, he carefully wrote "Disputation on the Power and Efficacy of Indulgences" across the top in his careful, scrolling script. Tomorrow morning he would take his list to the printer.

— ∎ —

Martin sat in his study late in the day on All Hallow's Eve, October 31, 1517. He dipped his quill pen in the dark black ink in front of him and began a letter to Archbishop Albert, the highest German authority to whom he could appeal.

May your Electoral Highness graciously permit me, the least
and most unworthy of men, to address you. The Lord Jesus
is my witness that I have long hesitated, on account of my
unworthiness . . .[10]

Martin looked up from his work and sighed. "Yet I must carry out what I now boldly do, moved by a sense of the duty I owe you[11]—as a priest. God help me with what I am about to do."

. . . What else can I do, right reverend father, than beg your
Serene Highness to carefully look into this matter . . . I could
be silent no longer . . . [12]

Martin finished his letter requesting that Albert hear his concerns before signing it:

If agreeable to your Grace, perhaps you would glance at my
enclosed theses, that you may see the opinion on the indul-
gences is a very varied one, while those who proclaim them
fancy they cannot be disputed.
  Your unworthy son, Martin Luther, Augustinian, set
apart as a Doctor of Sacred Theology
  Wittenberg[13]

Martin placed a copy of the newly printed *Ninety-Five Theses* behind his letter to Albert, carefully folding the papers and sealing them with wax from his candle. There was a knock on the door and Martin's friend Johann Schneider opened the door, ready and willing to stand beside Martin on the issue at hand. On the way through the Black Cloister, Martin arranged for his letter to be taken to

Archbishop Albert, and then the two men strode through the garden, past the college where groups of students discussed theology and philosophy, continuing down College Street. As they passed the market square, Martin shook his head at the crowds of people who had traveled from all the Saxon lands to see the relics in the Castle Church on All Hallow's Day. Martin knew that many would make their way from Wittenberg to find the monk Johann Tetzel so they could buy plenary indulgences that promised the forgiveness of their sins.

Martin and Schneider passed the home of the famed artist Lucas Cranach before exiting Wittenberg through the Schlosse Gate, which cut a decorative gash in the high city wall. The priest huffed as they trudged up the boarded walk that led to the main north door of the Castle Church. In medieval Germany, the heavy wooden door was the city's bulletin board.

Martin reached into the neckline of his hair shirt and removed a scrolled copy of the *Ninety-Five Theses*. With some ceremony, Schneider handed Martin a hammer and several rough nails. Martin unrolled the theses, held them to the door and beat a nail through the parchment into the wood behind. Over and over, he hit the hammer until his confrontational declaration was displayed for all to see.

As he hammered with all his might, Martin had no way of knowing that Pope Leo X and Archbishop Albert had agreed to split the profits of the indulgences. Nor did he know that Albert had purchased his church office from Leo. The little Wittenberg priest was unaware of the corruption and wild living in Leo's Rome. Martin just desperately hoped that these men would repair a wrong of which they were certainly not aware.

Ignorant to the importance of his actions, with every beat of his hammer Martin created shockwaves that were to travel through all of Germany, the whole of Europe, and the history of Christianity.

Chapter 12

FALLOUT!

November 1517–October 1518

Martin's footsteps crunched in the snow beneath his favorite pear tree. He winced as the frosty air bit at his lungs. Martin's midday meal of gruel sloshed in his stomach and his thoughts turned to his afternoon classes when he would preach on Galatians.

"Martin!" Andreas Karlstadt moved quickly across the university campus toward the Black Cloister. His black scholar's robe hung loosely from his broad shoulders and his short beard seemed to lead the way in front of his confident stride. Behind Andreas hurried a young, thin man with a prominent forehead and delicate, angular features. He had the look of a scholar too long at his books. "Martin,

I would like you to meet Doctor Philipp Melanchthon, the Greek scholar you have been asking for."

Martin looked over the young man head to toe. "How old are you, Philipp?"

"Twenty-one, Doctor."

Martin gave Melanchthon his most earnest glare until the young man flushed and examined his leather boots. "You sir, are a scrawny shrimp, much as I envision the apostle Paul."

There was an awkward silence as the young Greek scholar processed Martin's outburst. Martin's face twisted and then he laughed long and loud. "Welcome to Wittenberg, the stinking sand dune. It is high time you arrived, as I am much in need of counsel in the area of the Greek language."

Melanchthon's face slowly eased into a smile. "I hear you've made quite the impression, Doctor. Your *Ninety-Five Theses* have swept like a flame across all of Europe. In Heidelberg, the *Theses* were nailed to every street corner and building—even to the trees. I hear also that both the archbishop and the emperor know of your work and have written to the pope asking him to silence you."

Martin grimaced. "Yes, well, it is a mystery to me how my theses were spread to so many places. They were meant only for local debate."

Melanchthon laughed. "It is certainly a debate you are receiving."

"Not quite the debate I had hoped for. The printer must have saved a copy for himself and printed it in German. I was very careful to write the *Theses* in Latin." Martin glanced heavenward and sighed. "Since All Hallow's Eve, that fool monk Johann Tetzel," Martin spat. "Pig theologian! Tetzel treats the Scriptures as a sow pushes about a sack of grain.[1] He has threatened to have me burned and my ashes dumped in the Elbe. A Dominican abbot has been to the Black Cloister to frighten my monks, and Tetzel has written 106 countertheses against my points. He has accused me of heresy, which is punishable by death. The jester cannot even publish his own work as he is merely a monk, so he has used the name of his professor, Konrad Wimpina, as the author. I have, of course, written *Sermon on Indulgences and Grace* in response. This I have published in German for the common man to read."

Karlstadt elbowed Melanchthon. "Are you sure you wish to work with this rogue priest, Philipp?"

Melanchthon shifted his weight from foot to foot. "I am surely intrigued by the points made in the *Ninety-Five Theses*. You certainly appear to be a busy priest."

Martin laughed wryly. "Yes, you could say that I am busy."

Melanchthon's next thought was interrupted by a din coming from the direction of the market square. All three men turned toward the square as thick black smoke poured over the rooftops along the north side of College Street.

"Fire!" yelled Karlstadt as he began to run toward the square. Martin's footsteps fell hard on the frozen ground as he struggled to keep pace with the younger professors. As the men approached the square, the noise became louder and more chaotic. Students were hauling armfuls of booklets from a merchant's overturned cart and tossing them into the flames of a roaring bonfire. A group of young men in the gowns of scholars pushed a merchant before yelling threats at him, then shoving him again.

Martin crossed the market quickly, grabbing several students by their collars and throwing them back. "You! I demand you stop harassing this man."

"But Doctor, this man is selling Tetzel's *Countertheses.* We Germans are being robbed by the Roman church, and we will stand for it no longer!"

Martin rubbed the back of his neck and closed his eyes, hoping the chaos before him would disappear. "It is likely that I will be blamed for this mess by my enemies. You must all clean up the square and return to classes at once." Martin turned to the unfortunate book vendor. "I suggest you leave and do not return as tempers are high." The vendor nodded and ran for the Elbe Gate, abandoning his broken cart. The ashes of his books floated white and heavy through the air.

Martin turned to Melanchthon and Karlstadt with a frown. "Philipp, again I welcome you to Wittenberg."

━━ ▪▪ ━━

Martin looked over the council of Augustinian leaders in the convent at Heidelberg. Several of the younger men met his gaze with looks of understanding and even excitement. Many of the older priests shook their heads in disbelief.

April 25, 1518, was a chilly spring day. Martin's bones ached after his eleven-day journey to Heidelberg, most of it on foot, under threat of death from those who opposed his new ideas. As the district vicar, Martin had just given a speech to the council, explaining in detail that men are saved only by the grace of God—never by any work of their own doing.

"I have great hope," finished Martin, "that as Christ, when rejected by the Jews went over to the Gentiles, so this true theology, rejected by opinionated old men, will pass over to the younger generation."[2] Martin sat, hoping that some of his scriptural arguments would influence at least a few of the theologians in the room.

Martin's superior and dear friend Dr. Johann von Staupitz cleared his throat, causing his great fleshy jowls to shake. "Doctor Luther, we have received a number of letters of complaint against you. We ask that you take leave of us while we discuss how we might handle the situation. Thank you for your testimony."

Martin nodded. "I understand. And I resign my duties as vicar."

It was early May when Martin began the journey home. No decision had been made on how to deal with his "New Theology," but Martin's resignation was accepted. Though he walked to Heidelberg, he was invited to ride toward home in the cart of the Nuremberg delegates for as far as they could take him. As Martin prepared to enter the wagon, a young priest approached. Martin thought his prominent forehead, aggressively straight nose, and jutting chin caused him to resemble a bird of prey.

"Doctor Luther, I am Martin Bucer and this is Johannes Brenz. I must tell you that you were gracious in every response, and showed outstanding patience in listening.

Your knowledge of Scripture can rival only that of the apostle Paul. Also, I have never before heard the theology of the cross. I hope that I will read more of your thoughts in the coming months."

The champion of the New Theology thanked Martin Bucer and climbed into the wooden cart headed toward home. Along the way, Martin moved to the cart of the Erfurt delegation and on May 8, he stopped in Erfurt to speak with his beloved professor, Herr Trutvetter. The old man initially refused to see Martin, but gave in the following day. Martin carefully explained to Trutvetter the truth of the gospel, and the glorious revelation of Scripture. The old man just shook his head in sorrow over Martin's belief that all theology must come from the Bible itself. Martin left Erfurt on the wagon of the delegates from Eisleben, crestfallen that he had failed to show his aging professor the veracity of God's Word.

The priest arrived in Wittenberg on May 15. Martin was never idle, and he immediately wrote *Resolutions Concerning the Ninety-Five Theses*, an expanded explanation of each of his theses. In his scrolling handwriting he wrote:

> *The church needs a reformation. It is not the business of one man—namely the pope, or of many men—namely the cardinals. On the contrary, it is the business of the entire Christian world, yes, the business of God alone.*[3]

There was a sharp knock and Andreas Karlstadt opened the door to Martin's study. From behind Karlstadt, a richly dressed court herald pushed his way through the door. The man was stout and dark with an olive complexion. Martin recognized his look as that of the Italians he had seen upon his visit to Rome long ago. The warm August weather made the room stuffy and the shutters were thrown wide on the window. The herald stepped in front of the light from the opening and thrust a sealed parchment package at Martin. There, in the wax, was the emblem of the pope.

Martin took a deep breath. As the herald left the room, he unrolled the parchment to reveal a citation from Leo X. Picking up his quill, Martin penned a letter to his friend Georg Spalatin, the court chaplain of Prince Frederick the Wise.

> *I have been ordered to appear before the court in Rome in 60 days from today. This being the 7th of August, 1518. So you see, just how subtly and maliciously those preachers are working for my death![4] You must petition the Prince for a hearing in Germany, for in Rome I will certainly burn at the stake.*

Martin buried his head in his hands. "I believe the truth of Scripture," he said aloud. "And now I must die. Oh, what a disgrace I shall bring to my parents."[5]

Through the intervention of Prince Frederick the Wise, Martin was spared the certain death of a trip to Rome. Instead, he traveled to Augsburg to stand trial before

Cardinal Cajetan, leaving Wittenberg on September 26 with his fellow monk Leonhard Beier. Martin took with him letters of safe conduct from the prince, guaranteeing his safety. He knew the guarantee was in word only. The pair stopped three days later in Weimar, where Martin preached.

"You can stay in this cell," said the prior in the Weimar convent, cocking his head at Martin. "You know that it is foolhardy to travel to Augsburg. My dear Doctor, the Italians are learned men, and I am afraid you will not be able to maintain your cause before them: they will burn you on account of it."[6]

Martin spent a restless night before traveling to Nuremberg, where he was again discouraged from appearing before the Cardinal. By the time Martin and Beier entered the gate to the city on October 7, Martin could barely walk. "I am ill, Leonhard, and the sky appears to be spinning. All I can hear is the beat of the wings of the dragon. I am to die here in the devil's lair and I am too sick to fight as a true knight."

Beier helped Martin to the monastery where he lay sick for three days with a terrible stomach infection. During that time, the peasants milled about the monastery— hoping for a look at the famed priest. Noblemen who stood in support of Martin arranged for his care. Throughout his illness, Martin was plagued by the reoccurring question that rattled through his mind. *Are you alone wise?* It was a question he did not know how to answer. For indeed, the monk had set himself as wiser than even the pope!

— ■ —

Martin lay with his arms outstretched on the cold tile floor of the wealthy Fugger family. His nose and forehead pressed against the marble, and he remembered the day of his ordination as a monk. "Doctor Luther!" The ornately dressed cardinal seated in front of Martin was yelling and spit flew from his mouth, spraying droplets across his short, curly beard. His nose hooked sharply toward his mouth beneath wide-set eyes. Martin rose slowly to his knees. "I understand you to be a learned man. You are expected to recant of your errors and cease teaching them."

Martin swallowed hard. "Please, can you list for me my errors?"

Cajetan glared at the monk before him as if willing him to burst into flames on the spot. "Your first error is in saying that there is no bank of good deeds from the saints that would allow the purchase of indulgences. To think that the treasury of the church rests on the merits of Christ!" His voice dripped with icy condescension. "The second error is in stating that faith saves the sinner. It is actually the sacraments— the traditions of the church—that save. This new idea of yours is false."

The just shall live by faith, thought Martin. "I cannot concede the last point. We are saved by faith, and we are given faith through the grace of God."

"Recant. Admit your error; the pope wishes it so and not otherwise."[7] From the corners of the room, the cardinal's men jeered Martin, calling him names and laughing coarsely. "Your third error," continued Cajetan, "is to say that the authority of the pope is below the authority of a council, or . . ." Cajetan spat the word out. "Scriptures. Preposterous."

In spite of the rising voice of the cardinal and the jeers of his men, Martin refused to recant. Rather, he demanded to hear a scriptural reason for Cajetan's three points. The two men argued back and forth vainly. In anger, Cajetan had Martin forcibly removed from the hearing.

Martin's second meeting with Cajetan the following day did not go well. Though Martin apologized for his demanding behavior at their first meeting, and Cajetan promised to behave as a father, Martin still refused to agree that the pope had the authority to give indulgences. Martin knew the pope possessed no power to forgive sins. That was the work of Jesus Christ alone.

Martin brought documentation to his third meeting with Cajetan.

"I have found proof that a council is above the pope on matters of doctrine. Also, that faith is necessary before any traditions are meaningful, and that the Scriptures are above all humans. Men err."

Cajetan reached for the stack of parchment that Martin held and threw it aside. "Recant, my dear son."

Martin stared at the cardinal with a slack jaw. Cajetan pointed out that he, too, had stacks of paperwork from 1343, more than a thousand years after Jesus rose from the dead.

"You must agree to the doctrine of indulgences, Doctor Luther."

"O, most reverend Father, you state Christ acquired a treasure. Consider this word 'acquire.' If Christ by his merits acquired a treasure, then his merits are not the treasure, but that which the merits merited, namely, the keys of the church, are the treasure. Christ *is* the treasure. Do not think, most reverend Father, that we Germans understand no grammar; it is a different thing to acquire a treasure and to be a treasure."[8] Martin saw the look of frustration on the cardinal's face and tried a new tack. "May I write to you my statement? I have more to say on the subject of Holy Scripture and I do think we have wrangled quite enough."[9] *Surely if the cardinal is convinced of Scripture, he will agree with me. This must be a simple misunderstanding. All of this is written in the Bible for anyone to see.*

"My son, I did not wrangle with you. I am ready to reconcile you to the Roman church."[10]

Martin sighed. The cardinal had heard nothing during his three days of quoting Scripture. "I am not conscious of going against Scripture, the fathers, the decretals, or right reason. I may be in error. I will submit to the judgment of the universities of Basel, Freiburg, Louvain, and, if need be, of Paris."[11]

"Even Scripture must be interpreted. The pope is the interpreter." Cajetan had adopted the tone of a father explaining basic facts to a young child. "The pope is above Scripture, and above a council."

"His Holiness the pope abuses Scripture! I deny that he is above Scripture."[12] Martin glared at the cardinal. There was one King—Jesus. Scripture was God's Word, and no pope would ever rise above the Word of God. No longer were the two men arguing about indulgences. They were arguing about kingship.

Cajetan slammed his fist against his armrest and roared inches from Martin's face. "Go, and let me not see you again unless you recant."[13]

Martin left the hearing dejected and angry. Halfway down the hallway he turned on Staupitz in a rage. His mentor stood wringing his hands, waiting to hear news of the latest encounter with the cardinal. "Cajetan is a puzzle-headed, obscure, senseless theologian and Christian, as well fitted to deal with and judge this business as a donkey to play the harp."[14] Martin could feel foam forming at the corners of his lips. "I won't make myself a heretic by contradicting the opinion that made me a Christian. I will die first by fire, or be exiled and cursed."[15]

Martin remained in the monastery in Augsburg for more than a week while Staupitz and Prince Frederick met with Cajetan. During that time Staupitz released Martin from his vows as an Augustinian monk. It was a great sorrow to Martin to lose both his place as an Augustinian and his friendship with Staupitz. Martin wrote a letter to the pope complaining about the lack of scriptural support for indulgences, about Cajetan, and about how unsafe a journey to Rome would be. *If the cardinal here in Germany is unreasonable, it is only because the Holy Father does not know of it*, reasoned Martin.

Martin awoke in the dark with hands dragging him to his feet. By the position of the moon outside the window, he judged it was past midnight. "Martin. Martin, get up. You must leave now." He was pushed from his room and out a side door into the cold late October air.

"But I have no undergarments on," whispered Martin desperately. "I have nothing save my gown."

"There's no time," breathed the voice of a man near the bewildered reformer. "Hurry—to the wall of the city."

"But it's after dark. The gates will be closed and guarded carefully. I cannot leave even though I may wish to."

Herded through the winding streets of the city, Martin was out of breath when he reached the massive stone wall. He could barely make out a small chasm in the wall ahead. "Don't make me go in there!" he pleaded.

Martin was shoved roughly into the hole. He felt his way on his hands and knees across the jagged stone of the thick wall to the open air beyond and dropped to the ground with a thud. Without time to gain his bearings, he was grabbed and thrown atop a horse.

"NO! Do not make me ride this creature. I have no spurs. I have no undergarments . . . no sword. I shall be dashed to the ground—and my death. I have never before ridden a horse!"

"Quiet, monk." Out of the dark, Martin saw the flash of a whip. He grabbed the mane of the animal beneath him and hung on for dear life as the creature bolted across the fields outside Augsburg.

Chapter 13

CONTEST IN LEIPZIG

October 20, 1518–July 1519

Martin arrived in Nuremberg sore and bruised from his wild ride through the night and early hours of the morning. At the local convent, he was shown an order circulating from the pope. Should Martin refuse to recant, he was to be sent at once to Rome—in chains. Martin could not believe the order was correct. *This must all be a misunderstanding. Should Pope Leo X hear reason and logic from Scripture, he would certainly agree with me.*

It was All Hallow's Eve in 1518 when Martin finally returned home—exactly one year after the day he had nailed the *Ninety-Five Theses* to the door of the Castle

Church. Soon after, he received a letter from Prince Frederick, carried by a royal herald.

Martin hurried to his office in the tower of the Black Cloister. Settling into his wooden chair, he broke the wax seal on the parchment and began to read. Frederick had enclosed a letter from Cardinal Cajetan and he requested a response from Martin. Slowly, he pulled the cardinal's letter from behind Frederick's and began to read.

So, the prince is either to ban me from Saxony—or turn me over to Rome? Martin groaned aloud. *Surely the pope would understand my case if only I could present it before a council. He is a good pope. Not like that warrior pope before him, Julius II.* Martin knew that Pope Julius II had ruled that any appeal to a council without the permission of the pope was heresy. Heresy was punishable by excommunication, or by death. Excommunication was supposed to mean that a person was no longer a member of the Roman church—and no longer eligible for heaven. *I have been freed from the belief that salvation is subject to the whims of a pope!*

Martin made his decision. He would write a letter to Frederick explaining his New Theology. In it, he would point out that only Christ can forgive sin and that Scripture is above the words of any pope, council, or man. He would write a letter to the pope appealing to a general council. The pope was not well informed of Martin's case, so Martin would inform him.

While I'm at it, I'll write a pamphlet in German for the people. Martin dipped his quill in ink and began to scrawl on a stack of blank papers. *They must have an account of the meeting at Augsburg. They must know that the church is unwilling to debate me based on Scripture.*

It was later that day when Martin ran into Karlstadt on the way to the printer's shop.

"Martin, I have been searching for you. I have a letter from Prince Frederick's court priest Georg Spalatin. You are not to publish anything while the prince decides your fate."

Martin felt the old familiar burn of resentment rising within him. It took all he had to refrain from insulting those he hoped would help him. "Oh, Andreas, I wish that I had run into you sooner. I have just returned from the printer's and, alas, the deed is done. It is too late to stop my account of Augsburg."

Karlstadt's brow furrowed as he looked from the university behind them down College Street toward Mayor Street where the printer's shop resided. He looked Martin full in the face for several moments before slowly breaking into a boyish grin. "Well, God be with you then, my friend. May He go before you—before all of us who fight for the Word of God." With that, Karlstadt turned and walked back to the University of Wittenberg while Martin continued on to Mayor Street.

"Johann," Martin said to the printer, "I will need this account of my time in Augsburg published and distributed. I would also like copies of this letter to the pope. I do not want the letter distributed. I want to hold the copies for use if I should be banned. I plan to distribute them before I leave for France."

Martin's printer agreed to hold the letter to the pope for him until it was needed. Yet within hours, both the letter to the pope and the account of Augsburg were making their way across the country and down through Italy toward Rome itself, nailed to doors and trees in every small town and large city.

The days that followed were heavy with the silence from both the German prince of Saxony and from the pope and the cardinal of the Church of Rome. Martin continued to study Greek and Hebrew and to preach and lecture. He ceased teaching the words of several old philosophers and concentrated on teaching instead the truth of the Bible while he awaited the consequences of his actions. Daily, he expected to die for his faith.

By the end of 1518, Martin was prepared to leave his German home, believing France might be a good place for him to hide. Martin's old friend Staupitz, though not convinced of Martin's New Theology, sent a letter offering his home to the troubled priest.

Following his last sermon, Martin stood before the church filled with students, noblemen, and peasants. "I am an uncertain and unsettled preacher, as you have found out. How often have I left you suddenly without bidding you good-bye? If the same thing should ever happen again, in case I do not come back, I wish to say farewell to you."[1]

Martin returned to the Black Cloister where he had several of his friends over for supper before beginning his journey. He was midbite when a herald dressed in violet velvet and satin arrived. "Doctor Luther, I have a letter from Spalatin. You are to stay. Prince Frederick has committed to defend you and, as such, he has written to Cardinal Cajetan to demand a fair trial. Further, he has promised that there will be no trial outside of Germany, and no trial where you are not allowed to speak."

The herald turned to go. "Wait!" Martin ordered. Taking a quill and ink from the sideboard, he penned a note for Frederick.

I will willingly recant any article proved to me to be erroneous. For it is impossible to recant everything indiscriminately.[2]

Handing the letter to the herald, Martin excused himself. It was the perfect time to pray.

— ■ —

Through the winter and spring of 1519, Martin grew to see himself as a knight for the Lord, crusading against the great dragon of Rome. He ceased to see the pope as an ally or spiritual father and began to believe that the man in charge of the church had no interest in the gospel at all. In fact, Martin began to believe it quite possible that the pope himself was an agent of the dragon—if not the dragon himself.

As artists and printers grasped Martin's New Theology, cartoons and pamphlets began to circulate throughout Europe. The pope was made to look evil and silly; one cartoon showed the pope as a donkey attempting to play the bagpipes. The idea that Jesus Christ could save people from their sins without the permission of Rome grew in popularity.

It was during this time that Martin's close friend Johann Eck critiqued the *Ninety-Five Theses* in writing. Eck's analysis of Martin's work claimed that Martin was walking the line between heresy and rebellion. This diagnosis sparked a series of letters between Martin, Karlstadt, and Eck. Finally, the three agreed to debate at Leipzig University in the lands of Duke George, a bitter enemy of Martin's New Theology.

It was midday on Friday, June 24, 1519 when the Wittenberg delegates entered the town of Leipzig. Andreas Karlstadt rode alone in a rickety wagon ahead of the other men, surrounded by stacks of books he planned to use during the debate. Martin shared a cart with Philipp Melanchthon, the duke of Pomerania, and the rector of the University of Wittenberg. A group of some two hundred students and friends marched surrounding the caravan, brandishing spears, swords, and clubs.

"They have walked the whole forty-five miles south with us, Philipp," commented Martin.

"Yes. They are rowdy and create such a din. Yet they do desire to protect us on our journey."

"I'm not sure what use they may be against an army from Rome—or from the new boy-emperor in France."

There was a sharp cracking noise just ahead of the cart, like the sound of a dragon snapping its jaws closed on its helpless prey. Martin and Melanchthon strained to see through the crowd of students.

"It's Andreas!" cried Melanchthon. In horror, the two men watched as Karlstadt's cart tipped on end and collapsed to the side. The professor was tossed to the ground like a sack of barley, while his books nearly buried him in the muddy German road.

Martin sprang from the wooden slats he sat upon to pull Karlstadt from the ground. "Your wheel broke, Andreas," he whispered, shaken by the accident.

"My books." Karlstadt pulled his expensive tomes from the mud one at a time.

A nearby student surveyed the damage. "Well, this is a terrible omen." Others murmured their agreement.

"Nonsense. The Lord does not operate by omens and stars, regardless of what Philipp may claim." Martin fixed Melanchthon with a hard stare. He found the Greek scholar's affinity for astrology alarming. "Andreas, we must get you to a surgeon."

An hour later, Karlstadt allowed a doctor to bandage his arm while he eyed a basin full of his own blood. "It's strange, surgeon, but I feel worse after the bleeding than I did after the accident. I feel as though it may be difficult to think." The surgeon grunted and turned to Martin for payment.

━ ▪ ━

Martin sat in the audience of the debate between Karlstadt and Eck sniffing a small bouquet of wildflowers. *Karlstadt is doing quite well considering his accident and the quick, deceptive nature of Eck's arguments.* The priest approved of the manner in which Karlstadt clearly argued his case, supporting his thoughts with well-chosen passages from his beloved books. *To be certain, his voice seems more strained than usual and his temper quicker since the blood-letting.*

Outside the window, there were shouts and several crashes. Martin looked to the ceiling and sighed softly. His rowdy crowd of friends had been leaving town as their funds ran dry, but the remaining students often fought in Leipzig's taverns and made noisy retorts during the debate. Martin glanced around the room at the sixty-five Leipzig men who stood armed and ready to protect the debaters and those watching.

"I will not argue against a library,"[3] Eck roared.

Karlstadt raised his eyebrows. "I find a library most helpful in supplying arguments and citations from both the Scriptures and the church fathers, that I may not render them unrecognizable as you do."[4]

The gallery erupted with hissing and cheering from both sides. After some debate, Karlstadt was banned from consulting his books during the debate, which proved to be too harsh a requirement for him. Martin happily set down his bouquet of flowers and exchanged seats with Karlstadt.

Eck began. "Matthew 16:18 states: *'And I say also unto thee, that thou art Peter, and upon this rock I will build my church . . .'* Admit that Jesus placed the pope over the church. Anyone who denies the pope's supreme nature agrees with Jan Hus."

Martin thought back on the history of the church. "For one thousand years, the Greek church served God without any man claiming to be the head and without any link to Rome."

"And yet, Hus was sentenced to be burned at the stake by a council—not by a pope."

"Councils have erred. There have been times when councils condemned those things preached by Paul, or even by Christ."

At this point, Duke George stood. The crown of his bald head shone in the light from the windows, and his gray beard grazed the gold filigree along the collar of his gown. "What does it matter if the pope is leader by divine right or by human right? He remains the pope just the same."[5]

Martin considered the man's long gray mustache before replying. *The fact that God did not appoint the pope does not mean he should not be the head of the church. So long as he follows Scripture, he should be obeyed.* "Perfectly right."[6]

Eck interrupted. "The pope was pope from day one!"

Martin countered. "I believe the documents that you claim prove that statement—the decretals—were, in fact, forged."

For days, Martin and Eck argued about the pope, purgatory, and indulgences. Martin insisted there was no scriptural support for the existence of any of these institutions while Eck claimed they were all justified because past popes had declared them to be so.

Nearing the end of the debate, Eck closed his trap about Martin's neck. "Dr. Luther, your claims are dangerously close to those of the heretic, Jan Hus, who denied the authority of church councils, and the supremacy of the pope, the heir of Peter."

Martin flushed at the thought of being compared to a condemned heretic. Despite the alarm rising in his throat, he could not force himself to remain silent. "Among the articles of Jan Hus, I find many which are plainly Christian and evangelical, which the church cannot condemn."[7]

There was a gasp from the audience. Duke George lumbered to his feet once more. "That's the plague!"[8] The duke pointed a fattened finger at Martin.

"Are you the only one that knows anything?" erupted Eck. "With the exception of you, is all the church in error?"[9]

Martin felt control of the crusade slipping from him. Battle drums sounded in his ears, and the wing-beat of the dragon circling him thumped in time to the beating of his heart. Here again was the question that plagued him. *Are you alone wise?* It came to him in his dreams and assaulted him during sermons. It was the question he could not slay.

"I answer that God once spoke through the mouth of a donkey. I will tell you straight what I think. I am a Christian theologian. I am bound not only to speak the truth, but to defend the truth with my death and my blood. I want to believe freely and be a slave to the authority of no one, whether council, university, or pope. I will confidently confess what appears to me to be true, whether it has been asserted by a Catholic or a heretic."[10]

Again, the crowd gasped.

At the end of the debate both men were given a moment to speak. Martin looked out over the crowd, knowing that shortly after he left Leipzig, he would be officially declared a heretic, and his life would be forfeit. "I grieve that the Holy Doctor flees from the Scriptures as the devil from the cross. With all respect for the church fathers, I prefer the authority of the Scriptures. I recommend them to all."[11]

Eck snorted. "The impatient monk is more insulting than a theologian ought to be. He prefers the authority of Scripture to all of the church fathers. In so choosing, he sets himself up as a wise oracle—the only one with an understanding of the Scriptures superior to any Father."[12]

Martin closed his eyes, imagining his armor dented and broken. He had lost the battle, yet he'd had an opportunity to speak in defense of Scripture. *If I'm going to die, did I at least communicate how important the Bible truly is?*

Chapter 14

WAR OF WORDS

August 1519–December 1520

Martin watched as the last of the students left the lecture hall.

"It's astounding how many attend your classes these days, Martin." Philipp Melanchthon entered the room quietly, a stack of Greek books in his arms. "Almost as inspiring as the reach of your compilation book which contained the *Ninety-Five Theses*, *Resolution*, and several of your sermons. I hear it has spread to France, Spain, and England. Ulrich Zwingli in Switzerland has ordered several hundred copies and has a man on horseback giving them to people in villages far and wide! I hear that you have even received a letter from a former student in Rome stating that he's risking death by giving away your books right under the nose of the pope!"

"That's true; I have received a letter from my student in Rome. I must agree, it's astounding to see the number of students attending Wittenberg. I am quite certain they are drawn by your excellent book on the grammar of the Greek language, Philipp."

Melanchthon laughed as he set down his books. "More likely your debate skills at Leipzig nearly a year ago, Martin. You have not only stated the truth of Scripture—you have drawn the church into discussion. Perhaps we can be reconciled with the pope after all. We desire unity, do we not?"

"My die is cast. I despise the fury and favor of Rome—I will never be reconciled to them nor commune with them. Let them condemn and burn my books!"[1]

"Martin, you are too easily offended, and your temper rules you on occasion, I fear."

"But you, Master Philipp, walk softly and silently, till and plan, sow and water with pleasure, as God has gifted you richly. And Karlstadt is hotter in the matter than I."[2]

At this, Melanchthon nodded his head. "Yes, Andreas's passion for reforming the church exceeds mine. I fear he broke with Rome long before you. I hear, too, that you have reduced the sacraments to only three: baptism, confession, and the Lord's Supper. It seems as though now that you have started your reforms, there will be no end!" Melanchthon fingered a paper that lay atop his leather-bound stack of papers. "Oh! Martin, I have forgotten the reason for my visit. You have received a letter from that humanist Ulrich von Hutten. He supports you fully, you know, and even proposes the use of force. I hear he has the knight Franz von Sickingen standing at the ready, with a hundred knights in Von Sickingen's castle—they desire to defend you."

Martin opened the papers Melanchthon handed him and began to read aloud.

> *Honorable Doctor Luther, It is said that you are under the ban of the Church. If this is so, how great are you, Luther, how great! . . . But beware! You see that if you fall it will be a great injury to the State, but I know from your actions that you are resolved to die rather than merely live. . . . Be strong! But why should I admonish you when I have no need? In any event you have a supporter in me and may confide your plans to me. . . . If God be for us, who can be against us?*[3]

Martin continued reading before glancing at Melanchthon. "He has also urged me to allow him to send his one hundred knights to defend me in my travels and at home. I am not offended by his offers to assist me. Doubtless this will happen unless God interposes. But I doubt not that the Lord will accomplish his purpose through me—though I am a foul sinner—or through another."[4]

Melanchthon's brow wrinkled. "Martin, what of the excommunication? Are you not concerned of the news that you will be barred from the church—and from heaven?"

Martin laughed. "The pope does not have the jurisdiction to ban me from heaven. Only Christ has that task. I will stand alone before Him alone. I have been condemned by the universities of Louvain and Cologne, and the pope's bull is rumored to excommunicate me. We will pay no more attention to their condemnation than to the silly ravings of a drunken woman."[5]

— ▪ —

The late summer and fall of 1520 were busy for Martin. In August he wrote *Address to the Christian Nobility*, in which he petitioned the German princes to take the leadership of the church from Rome. He desired to see the reforms he started be instituted. Martin's attacks on the church of Rome were becoming more pronounced. He called the pope, cardinals, and bishops "ravening wolves who come dressed in sheep's clothing" and the pope's officials a "crawling mass of reptiles." Martin also stated that ordained priests were not special, but that there is a priesthood of all believers—every follower of Christ has access to the grace of God. Copies of *Address to the Christian Nobility* sold out in two weeks' time.

On the 10th of October, nearly three years after Martin nailed the *Ninety-Five Theses* to the door of the church, he was walking through the market square when he noticed a rowdy crowd around one of the pillars supporting the covered deck used for making announcements. As Martin approached the pillar, the townspeople parted to make way for him. Taped to the post was an official bull, signed by Pope Leo X. Martin cleared his throat and in his best speaking voice, began reading aloud:

> *Arise, Lord, plead thine own cause. Arise and protect the vineyard thou gavest Peter from the wild boar who is devouring it.*[6]

Martin flushed. *I am a wild boar, am I? Oh, and the pope calls me a heretic. Well, I call him antichrist, for surely he stands against Jesus.* He scanned the rest of the document before reading the end:

> *We can no longer suffer the serpent to creep through the field of the Lord. The books of Martin Luther which contain these errors are to be examined and burned.*[7]

A traveling merchant peeked over Martin's shoulder. "Aye, the good man has sixty days to respond before he is excommunicated. I see his books being burnt in city after city. Though in several cities, the men posting copies of this bull were nearly stoned. That'll leave a bruise, friend, those stones will." He laughed.

"It is not real!" exclaimed Martin suddenly. "It is better that I should die a thousand times than that I should retract one syllable of the condemned articles. And as they excommunicated me for the sacrilege of heresy, so I excommunicate them in the name of the sacred truth of God." Martin waved his arm as a knight lifting his sword to declare victory. The crowd began to cheer. "Christ will judge whose excommunication will stand. Amen."[8]

With that, the wild boar turned and stomped toward College Street. Over the din of the crowd, he heard the merchant say, "Aye, so that would be the great Martin Luther, then?"

A week and a half later, Martin published *Babylonian Captivity of the Church.* In it, the threatened priest claimed that only baptism and the Lord's Supper are required to follow Christ. Martin also argued that every believer—not just the priests—should be able to drink the wine during communion. Confession was helpful to believers, he asserted, but not necessary. Martin also claimed that the priests held all Christians captive with their insistence on seven sacraments. He attacked the idea that good works were needed to earn salvation. Finally, Martin claimed that every man and woman was saved based on their faith. No one could have faith for them.

In November the knight Franz von Sickingen wrote, offering to send knights to protect Martin. Rather than respond to von Sickingen, Martin wrote to the pope in one last attempt to ask him for an audience with a council. That month, Martin published *On the Freedom of a Christian*. He claimed that the Christian is free, but also a servant to everyone. Anyone who truly loves Jesus will serve those around him. However, serving others will never save anyone's soul. Martin also emphasized the importance of the Bible, writing:

> *One thing, and one alone, is necessary for life, justification, and Christian liberty; and that is the most holy Word of God, the Gospel of Christ . . .*[9]

It was eight-thirty on the morning of December 10 when Melanchthon opened the door to Martin's cell in the Black Cloister. Martin looked up from his knees and struggled to raise his bony frame. "Is it time, Philipp? I must have been long in prayer."

"You were, Martin. I have posted your decree on the door of the Castle Church, and now we must go."

The two professors walked silently from the Black Cloister to the Elster Gate. Melanchthon pulled the large wooden cart Martin had piled high with tomes of the laws and decisions of the Catholic Church. Martin had added books of theology to the pile, tossing the writings of his former friend Johann Eck right on top. As he crossed the wooden drawbridge over the rancid moat surrounding Wittenberg, the smell of the stockyards cut the chill air with the pungent scent of death. Martin had accepted his coming execution as inevitable. In only twenty-four days, he would be excommunicated as a heretic, and his life would become open sport for anyone who wished to take it.

The joyful sound of students and peasants singing shook Martin from his reverie.

> *We praise thee, O God:*
> *we acknowledge thee to be the Lord.*
> *All the earth doth worship thee:*
> *the Father everlasting.*
> *To thee all Angels cry aloud:*
> *the Heavens, and all the Powers therein.*
> *To thee Cherubim and Seraphim:*
> *continually do cry,*
> *Holy, Holy, Holy:*
> *Lord God of Sabaoth;*
> *Heaven and earth are full of the Majesty*
> *of thy glory.*[10]

Down on the bank of the Elbe, where the carcasses of slaughtered cattle and the clothing of the diseased were normally burnt, a bonfire licked toward heaven. A triumphant cry went up from the crowd when they spotted

Martin crossing the sandy turf. Martin held up his hands for quiet and waited for a few moments.

Just as the students began to look restless, the priest pulled from his hair shirt the long papal bull which declared him to be a heretic and scheduled his excommunication. Shaking it open, Martin glared at the document. The peasants stifled giggles when Martin began to speak to the paper.

"Because you have brought down the truth of God," Martin addressed the papal bull as though he were an executioner at its final judgment. All around him, he could feel the wind of battle and the screech of circling dragons, their hot breath nearly scalding his face. "God also brings you down into this fire today. Amen!"[11] With that, Martin hurled the bull onto the pyre. A guttural roar went up from the crowd, like the cry of men in battle once they have committed to fight to the death.

Melanchthon quickly handed Martin the laws of the Roman Catholic Church. The priest heaved the heavy tome with all his might and it lumbered through the air before crashing to the wood below, sending sparks cascading into the crowd. Men from all sides descended on the cart beside Martin. Many commentaries explaining the laws and traditions of the church were burned that day. The priest smiled when he saw several of the tomes written by Johann Eck among the flames, their yellowed pages curling and buckling between the leather covers.

As the fire softened and the war cries subsided, Martin made his last speech of the day. "Since they have burned my books, I burn theirs." Again, the men around the fire erupted into cheers and whistles. Martin raised his voice. "The canon law is included because it makes the pope a god on earth. So far I have merely fooled with this business of the pope. Seldom has the pope overcome anyone with Scripture and reason."[12]

Martin turned on his heel and marched toward the Elster Gate, followed closely by the other university professors. Behind him, students threw more and more shingles upon the flames, pushing the fire higher and higher. That night, they would celebrate their stand against the pope far into the late hours. Martin last heard the wild crowd singing a funeral song in Hebrew as they prepared for a parade through the streets of the town.

Chapter 15

WELCOME TO WORMS

January 1521–May 1521

Martin glanced around at the men in the carriage provided by a wealthy friend from Wittenberg. Andreas Karlstadt sat next to him. Across from Martin and Karlstadt sat Professor Nicolaus von Amsdorf. The men were accompanied by a Wittenberg monk and a student. With a sigh, Martin contemplated his death. He spoke aloud to himself, justifying his actions.

"I will go if I possibly can—I will go ill if I cannot go well. For it is not right to doubt. If I am summoned by the emperor, I am summoned by the Lord. He lives and reigns who saved the three Hebrew children in the furnace of the king of Babylon. If he does not wish to save me, my life is a little thing compared to that of Christ . . ."[1]

Amsdorf frowned, deep lines of anxiety creasing their way down his face like raindrops down a cloak. Martin turned away and gazed across the countryside leading the way to the city of Worms. The men had been traveling for days on their way to the Diet of Worms, the council in which the Holy Roman Emperor, the German princes, and the Roman church officials would meet. Throughout their travels, Martin had preached to massive crowds. In Erfurt, he had stopped his sermon when the creaking of the upper balcony had sent alarm through the congregation. "Be still, dear people. It is only a joke of the devil. Be still—there is no danger,"[2] he had promised, hoping it was true. Across Germany, peasants, knights, and noblemen alike had thronged to the road to cheer the priest onward toward his meeting with Emperor Charles V of the Holy Roman Empire.

Amsdorf drew a breath. "Perhaps you could still flee to France?" The professor's tone was hopeful.

"Here is no place to weigh risk and safety!" stormed Martin. "We must take care not to abandon the gospel which we have begun to preach. It is certainly not for us to determine how much danger to the gospel will accrue by my death."[3] Martin pounded his palm with his fist. He imagined what it would be like to die. Death would be an honor, if it was for God, his King.

Karlstadt scowled at Martin. "Well, I have no intention of dying. We will be victorious! We have the people on our side, the princes of Germany on our side—well, many of

them, the knights of Sickingen and Hutten on our side—
you know we could still go to Ebernburg Castle and be well
protected while we negotiate with the papists. Just because
you've been excommunicated, it does not mean that we
must surrender all hope of life."

Erfurt rose in the distance before the party like a great
beast taking flight. Kaspar Sturm, the imperial herald of
Emperor Charles, rode his tall steed several yards ahead
of the carriage. Blades of sun shone off the golden eagle
pinned to Sturm's arm, leaving little circles of light swirl-
ing in Martin's eyes. Whipping around on Karlstadt, he
bellowed, "Truly Christ lives and I shall enter Worms in
the face of the gates of hell and the princes of the air."[4] He
softened. "Truth be told, I have had my Palm Sunday. Is
all this pomp merely a temptation, or is it also a sign of the
passion to come?"[5]

Martin pondered his own words. *Lord, save me from
pride. I speak well of my desire for a fight, but do I really feel
this way? Can I be martyred well?*

Martin's musing was punctuated by a loud trumpet
call. The early morning sun shone on the heads of horses
and their men as they galloped across the Rhine River
toward the small party from Wittenberg. "Why, there must
be a hundred or more horsemen riding toward us!" Amsdorf sounded awed and afraid. Martin thought he could
make out the glint of hard steel waving in the air.

There was nothing to do but watch as the horsemen galloped toward the little group of men in their carriage with
only a sole imperial herald to guard them. Thirty minutes
later, Sturm shouted courageously from his steed. "Ho! We

are under the guarantee of safety from the emperor. You are not to harm these men."

The lead horseman laughed in a strong, mirthless voice, his sword drawn. "Harm them? We are here to guard them!" Hooves swirled in circles about the carriage as Martin and his companions were enveloped in a cloud of sweaty horsehair, dusty linen, and creaking leather. The smell was nearly overwhelming. "Welcome to Worms, Doctor Luther. You will find the city crowded—most homes have six or seven sleeping in a bed, and I hear that even the emperor shares his room with his chief advisor. We are all excited and honored to have you join us."

The carriage was swept along and by eleven o'clock in the morning, as the procession was clopping across the bridge to the city, Martin could hear nothing but the cheers and calls of people. "Long live Luther." The chant was deafening, punctuated only by the occasional "Down with Rome!"[6]

As the carriage reached the gate, Karlstadt leaned over to whisper to Martin, his face flushed with excitement. "We will not even be able to squeeze through. There are so many here who love you."

The horsemen were forced to fall into line before and aft the carriage. Peasants crushed so close to the side, Martin feared they would be swept beneath the wheels and injured. From every window and perch in the wall of the city, from every window lining the streets, and from every tree limb along the cobblestone roads, people stretched to wave to Martin cheering always, "Long live Luther!"

Out of a tavern far ahead, a group of Spaniards dressed in their finest overturned a cart of books. Martin could see them pushing the merchant and slapping his face. He took a deep breath as he saw one begin to draw his sword. Suddenly, the Spanish knights were mobbed by city peasants in defense of the harried bookseller. As the carriage made its way down the narrow roadway, Martin saw the Spaniards escape from the mob with their colorful tunics shredded and blood running down their faces. The knights raced toward their lodging where they would be protected by their brethren.

As the carriage passed the site of the mauling, Karlstadt leaned over the side to investigate. His voice rose in excited confidence. "The merchant is ruffled but will recover. The books were all yours, Martin."

Martin turned to look back on the scene while another scuffle broke out on his left between an Italian cardinal and a German nobleman. Martin shuddered. "God will be with me."[7]

— ∎ —

Around four o'clock on the following afternoon, April 17, 1521, Karlstadt opened the door to the cell he was sharing with the other men from Wittenberg and nodded to Martin. "It is time, friend."

Martin followed the imperial herald Kaspar Sturm and the imperial marshal through the garden of the Augustinian monastery to the back stairway of the bishop's palace.

The men waited silently until Sturm received a signal from the stairway. "Come," he said.

Martin trudged up each step with a growing feeling of dread. Through the open windows of the staircase, he could hear the shouted anger of the people below as the fights between the Spaniards and the Germans spilled into the streets. The imperial marshal held the heavy oak door for Martin and the priest entered a room packed with standing spectators. The smell of manure and sweat nearly caused Martin to heave. He pressed his hands to his stomach in an effort to keep his midday meal from escaping. Down the long corridor before him, the emperor was seated on a long, raised platform. Charles V was surrounded by his royal Spanish advisors, and Roman cardinals, bishops, and administrators sat in positions of authority. Flanking the platform, Charles's armed guard stood at attention, dressed in their finest uniforms. Between Martin and the officials stood a wooden table piled high with books, and a well-dressed church representative waited beside it.

Martin walked past the throng of noblemen, his heart sinking deeper into his belly with every step. Groups of Spaniards hissed and booed while German nobility sat quietly, eying the cause of unrest in their territories. Martin searched the faces before locating that of his protector, Prince Frederick the Wise. Frederick returned Martin's glance without indication of warmth or compassion.

In a loud, clear voice, the church representative— the chancellor of the archbishop of Trier—began the hearing. "Martin Luther, the emperor and realm have summoned you hither, that you may say and tell them whether you have composed these books, and others which bear your name."[8]

Martin looked at the pile of material in front of him. "I have written those." He was surprised that his voice would not come forth with more force or volume.

"And secondly, that you may let us know whether you propose to defend and stand by these books."[9] The chancellor looked impatient.

From behind Martin a well-dressed man stepped forward. "I am Doctor Schurff, Doctor Luther's lawyer. Let the titles of the books be read.[10] Let Doctor Luther be certain."

The chancellor heaved an irritated sigh and began. "*Address to the Christian Nobility, On the Babylonian Captivity of the Church, Lectures on Galatians, Lectures on Hebrews, The Ninety-Five Theses, Resolutions . . .*"

As the chancellor droned on, Martin began to feel faint. A trickle of sweat ran down the back of his head and pooled at the neckline of his cloak. Through his mind ran the old question which plagued him. *Are you alone wise?*

Martin interrupted the chancellor, panic rising in his soul. It was one thing to write passionate attacks from his quiet office in the tower, but to stand before these men and speak was another matter entirely. "This concerns faith and the salvation of souls and the Divine Word. It would be rash and dangerous to say anything without due consideration. I might say more or less than I should, either of which would bring me in danger of the sentence of Christ, and as he said, 'Whoso shall deny me before men, him will

I also deny before my Father in heaven.'" Martin brushed a hand across his eyelids to keep the sweat from stinging his sight. "I humbly beg your Imperial Majesty to grant me time for deliberation, that I may answer without injury to the Divine Word or peril to my soul."[11]

A roar of disbelief erupted from the platform in front. The young emperor stood to his feet and was quickly joined by a circle of his advisors. The chancellor gaped at Martin, disdain dripping from his voice like saliva from the tongue of a serpent about to feast. "You request more time? You have had months—no, years—to defend your position, O professor, O doctor of theology."

Holding his hand for silence, Charles V spoke. "Go now. You will return tomorrow. Then, Doctor Luther, you *will* answer me."

— ■ —

Martin spent a long night in prayer before writing across a stray piece of paper. "Truly, with Christ's aid, I shall never recant one jot or tittle."[12]

The following evening, Martin entered the great hall in candlelight and sharply drew his breath as he saw the volume of people in the room. Only the emperor sat upon his throne; all else stood, every man pressed against five other men as they waited to hear the German priest respond to the greatest powers on earth. Martin walked with his shoulders held back and his chin jutting so far that it looked as though he leaned backward toward the floor.

The chancellor lost no time. "Do you wish to defend all of your books," he made a sweeping motion toward the table, "or to retract part of them?"[13]

Martin began in a clear, calm voice, his nerves and resolve steadied by the hours he had spent in prayer. "Most Serene Emperor, Most Illustrious Princes, Most Clement Lords—if, by my inexperience, I should fail to give anyone the titles due him, please forgive me, as a man who has lived not in courts but in monastic nooks. The books are mine, as I published them. In reply to the second question from yesterday, be pleased to consider that all my books are not of the same kind. In some I have treated piety, faith, and morals so simply and evangelically that my adversaries themselves are forced to confess that these books are useful, innocent, and worthy to be read by Christians. Those I cannot undertake to recant."[14]

Martin wiped his forehead with his sleeve. "The second class of my work speaks against the papacy—laws of the pope and the doctrines of men—which has laid waste to all Christendom, body and soul. If I should withdraw these books, I would be the tool of iniquity and tyranny."[15]

Charles rose from his throne in a rage. "No!"[16] He punched the air with his index finger.

Martin envisioned a knight taking on not only an army of dragons, but the head dragon himself. "The third class of books I have written against some private individuals. In these I confess I was more bitter than is becoming to a minister of religion. Yet neither is it right for me to recant what I have said in these, for then tyranny and impiety would rage and reign against the people of God more violently than ever."[17]

The chancellor paced, looking every moment more like a snake recoiled and ready to strike. Martin fought the urge to step back. The chancellor dropped all pretense of civility, and he did not utter the title "Doctor" again. "Luther, you have not answered to the point. You ought not to call into question what has been decided and condemned by councils. Therefore I beg you to give a simple, unsophisticated answer without horns. Will you recant or not?"[18]

Martin narrowed his eyes. "Since your Majesty and your Lordships ask for a plain answer, I will give you one without either horns or teeth. Unless I am convicted by Scripture or by right reason—for I trust neither in popes nor in councils, since they have often erred and contradicted themselves—unless I am convinced, I am bound by the texts of Scripture. My conscience is captive to the Word of God. I neither can nor will recant anything, since it is neither right nor safe to act against conscience. God help me. Amen."[19] Martin threw his arms in the air as he imagined a knight would celebrate upon slaying the dragon.

The chamber hall erupted. The emperor was again on his feet, yelling at his advisors. Princes shouted at each other and Spanish troops bellowed and spat in the candlelight. Cries of "To the fire with him!"[20] rose to blend with the smoke of the candles.

Martin slipped out of the room and down the stairs, retreating to the silence of his cell. As he crossed the monastery garden, the city of Worms chanted. Cries of "Long live Luther!" met the shouts of "To the fire with him!" in the air, battling for victory. Martin found himself shouting in joy, "I am through! I am through!"[21]

— ■ —

The next morning the city of Worms awoke to a poster with a peasant's clog printed in the middle tacked to the door of the town hall. On the door where Emperor Charles was staying, a sign read: "Woe unto the land whose king is a child!"[22] Over the next eight days, the clog posters seemed to multiply and spread until they were found in every corner of the town. Supporters of the Roman Catholic Church knew the signs meant that peasants were threatening to revolt, and responded by posting signs of their own.

Martin received visits and calls to meetings, even bribes. Still he refused to recant. In frustration, Charles V sent Martin home with twenty-one days of safe conduct, ordering him to preach to no one on the way. Martin left with his friends on the morning of April 26, 1521. The imperial herald Kaspar Sturm led a small troop of guards sent to protect Martin until Wittenberg. Eager to be alone with his friends, Martin sent the herald and his troops back to Worms two days later with a letter for the emperor:

> *I am most ready to submit to and obey your Majesty—either in life or in death, to glory or in shame, for gain or for loss. As I have offered myself, thus I do now, in every area save the Word of God, as it is above all things. Scripture ought to be held free and unbound in all, as Paul teaches. It ought not to depend on human judgment nor to bend to the opinion of men.*[23]

It was the morning of May 4 when Martin, his fellow professor Nicolaus von Amsdorf, a monk, and a carriage driver left the village of Möhra where Martin had visited with his grandmother and uncle. Martin had preached at towns along the way and enjoyed seeing his family, but his twenty-one days of safe passage were marching onward with or without the little company of men from Wittenberg. Martin's uncle rode a horse beside the carriage, followed by family members and friends on horseback. At the Castle Altenstein, Martin signaled the driver to stop.

"Uncle Heinz, I have enjoyed seeing you."

"And I, you." His uncle shielded his eyes and gazed into the forest of Waltershausen. Martin followed his stare into the darker recesses of the wooded passageway. Light filtered through the dense canopy of trees before resting upon large bushes, not quite highlighting the undergrowth. "Martin, you will have to take the Gotha Highway through the forest. Would you like us to escort you?"

"No, Uncle, we will be fine. Thank you for the visit." Again, Martin desired to be alone with his friends, his thoughts, and his prayers.

The men shook hands and Martin's carriage rolled onward into the dark woods, past the castle's empty chapel. Martin turned to watch his uncle and family ride toward home. When he could see nothing but the dust from the horses' hooves in the air, he swiveled forward just in time to catch sight of a band of armed horsemen bearing down upon the carriage from a bend in the road ahead. The cart's horses reared as the bandits surrounded the carriage, yelling and kicking up dust.

"Where is Martin Luther?" one of the masked men shouted.

At the same moment, Martin's friend the monk bolted from the carriage and ran in the direction of Waltershausen. The driver turned with a look of horror etched across his face and pointed to Martin.

Chapter 16

KIDNAPPED!

May 1521–Spring 1522

N o!" shouted Amsdorf, standing between Martin and the lead horseman.

"Nicolaus, sit down." Martin struggled to help his friend to his seat. A nearby bandit pointed a crossbow at Martin while another hit Amsdorf across the face with the butt of his sword.

Martin felt strong hands close around his shoulders and pull him roughly out of the wagon. In a last burst of defiance, the priest grabbed the Hebrew Old Testament and Greek New Testament from the seat next to him before falling from the coach and landing roughly on the ground. Two of the men reached down to grab Martin by the elbows before galloping off around the bend in the highway. Martin clung to his books as his feet twisted and scraped against the ground between the two horses.

Once the wagon was out of sight, the bandits released Martin. He fell to the packed dirt road, wincing at the pain.

"Wear this." Martin was hit across the back of the head with the leggings and tunic of a knight.

"But I am a priest," sputtered Martin. His protest was met by the lowering of a crossbow in his direction. "And now I am a knight—with a tonsure. I am certain that is believable." In spite of himself, Martin dressed quickly.

"Ride this horse." One of the armed men dragged a horse from behind a tree.

"Oh, I do not wish to ride another horse!" cried Martin. He glanced back to see, again, the wicked end of a crossbow. Martin scrambled to the back of the mare with a few good pushes from his abductor.

The men rode through the woods for hours, up one little side trail and then down another. It was well after dark and the moon was high in the sky when Martin spotted Eisenach. He thought of his school days there, tutoring the son of Heinrich Schalbe. As the little troop of men turned their horses toward Wartburg Castle, Martin recalled thinking that the castle looked like a dragon, ready to pounce on some unsuspecting monk.

As he crossed the drawbridge of the castle and was hustled up tower stairs into a locked prison cell, Martin collapsed beneath the flutter of disturbed bats. *I was right. The Dragon Wartburg has indeed devoured a poor, unwilling monk.*

— ■ —

After a night of deep, motionless sleep, Martin awoke to find himself not in a prison cell, but in a small living room with a little sleeping chamber off to the side. The walls, ceilings, and floors were lined with worm-eaten wood panels and a square window sat in the exterior wall. The monk's tights and tunic rustled as he moved. He felt some embarrassment over the immodesty of his new garments, but was surprised by how comfortable they were—nothing like the hair dress he was accustomed to wearing. Martin stuck his head out and looked around. *I am in the region of the birds!*[1] The tower room looked out over the rolling hills above Eisenach. By leaning out a little way, Martin could see the brick exterior of the tower. Past the tower, the castle's white plaster walls and dark wooden accents stretched across the low mountain.

The priest rubbed his bony frame as he searched for the exit. A curved wooden door led to the only way out—a staircase surrounded by iron bars and chains. The staircase itself was rolled up to become part of the floor and it appeared that it would extend only to allow the warden into the cell. *I am a singular prisoner—who remains here not only voluntarily, but also involuntarily. Voluntarily, because my Lord wills it thus—involuntarily because I would gladly preach the Word of God among the people. I would rather burn upon glowing coals for the honor of God's Word than rot here alive.*[2]

Martin moved quickly back from the chains when he heard the stairs begin to creak and moan. Slowly, the structure unrolled and descended. The monk heard heavy footsteps moving toward him. He had a vision of a winged serpent ascending the stairs.

"Aye, up there. It is only me, the warden of your cell." An older man with a jolly face appeared, holding a plate of meat and pastries. "I thought ye may be hungry. This is the best I can do on such short notice. Welcome to the Wartburg."

Martin sniffed. "If I'm so welcome, remove the chains."

"Ah, I cannot do that. I'm to bring ye what ye'd like, but until your hair and beard grow out, ye cannot leave the castle. Even then, ye can only leave for short walks."

"By whose order?" Martin was angry.

The warden smiled a crooked grin. Where he had teeth remaining, the black roots peeked through his graying mustache. "By the order of Prince Frederick the Wise, Knight Jörg. I'm to keep ye here until he orders otherwise."

Martin straightened his sore back. "I am Martin Luther, and I demand to be let go. I have business to attend to."

The warden placed the breakfast plate at Martin's feet and lost his smile. "Ye are confused, Knight Jörg. Martin Luther is a heretic and an outlaw. His life is over—and the people believe he was killed by a mob of evil bandits. Ye are a nobleman and a knight. Ye may not look like one yet, but ye will once yer hair grows out. Let me know if ye need anything." The warden turned to leave.

Martin gathered his wits. "I need paper," he called out. "And ink. Quills—I need quills." The warden grunted on his way down the stairs. Martin nearly wept as the stairs folded back up into the floor beyond the chain.

It was weeks before Martin used his precious paper and ink. Deeply depressed, he read his Hebrew Old Testament, his Greek New Testament, and eventually he wrote letters to everyone he knew. Slowly, Martin's tonsure disappeared as his dark hair cascaded down his back. His beard grew full and wiry.

After years of fasting, the rich food of the castle made Martin terribly ill, and some days his stomach hurt so bad he wished to die. The priest found himself wishing for the torture of martyrdom rather than the long slow rot of sitting in a cell. After two months, Martin decided that if he was to be banished to live among the birds, just as Saint John was banished to the Isle of Patmos, he might as well work. And work Martin did.

For ten months Martin wrote. He penned a commentary on Psalm 68, and a commentary on Mary's song after John the Baptist leapt for joy in Elizabeth's womb. Martin composed a book about whether the pope can require ordinary everyday people to confess their sins to a priest; he taught that there is a priesthood of believers and that ordinary people can confess their sins to other ordinary people. He drafted a book about marriage and the clergy in which he argued that there is nothing in the New Testament that sets priests apart from ordinary people. Martin said marriage is allowed for everyone. He wrote a book about monastic vows, claiming that there is no such thing in Scripture.

The spring turned to summer and summer became fall. Martin received letters from across Europe. For every attack against his own character, Martin wrote an attack against the author. Martin's words were harsh and his insults and name-calling became legendary.

Letters from Wittenberg told the story of an encroaching chaos. Martin's anger grew as he realized the reformation of the church was marching forward without him, and he had no control over the path it was taking. Andreas Karlstadt was preaching in the little Thuringian town, and he was determined to push forward changes to the church as fast as he could dream them up.

—— ·· ——

Martin laid down a letter from his friend, the court clergyman Spalatin, and buried his head in his hands. His thick hair fell round his fingers and trickled down his forearms, startling him. It was December 2, 1521, and the chains had long ago been removed, allowing him to take long walks each day. Standing, Martin paced the room, noticing that his bony frame was now well padded. A sharp pain shot through his stomach. Martin had taken to talking aloud and as he stormed in small circles, he counted Wittenberg's changes on his fingers. "Monks and nuns are marrying, they are leaving the monasteries and convents, arrests have been made, all receive both the bread and the wine during the Lord's Supper, private masses have been banned, there are no vigils or masses for the dead, meat is eaten on fast days, and the university is failing because the sponsors are withdrawing their money. Something must be done. I shall take a longer morning walk today. In fact, I will borrow a horse from the stables. I'm sure no one will mind its absence." Martin had no intention of staying in Eisenach when he was needed in Wittenberg.

Martin strapped on his sword and walked to the stairs. He rode his "borrowed" horse hard through the countryside, arriving in Wittenberg in only two days. The town church was a mess. "What happened here?" he asked a passerby.

The man looked the strange knight up and down. "It was a riot, sir. The students and some of the townspeople went in with knives and took the mass books and ran off the priests. They threw stones at the people praying to the Virgin Mary. My wife was at Mass here, and she has a nasty bump on the back of her head." He lowered his voice. "If you ask me, half the people in this town are going to hell. The other half are just hoping for things to return to the way they were." The man nodded his head and moved onward, muttering to himself.

Martin gazed at the altar covered in rocks before shaking his head. Heading up the street, he paused before the house of Nicolaus von Amsdorf. Martin knew that Philipp Melanchthon was renting a room from Amsdorf and he decided to have some fun. Straightening his tunic and running his fingers through his flowing hair and beard, he knocked on the door with a flourish.

Amsdorf answered. "Yes?"

"I have come for a visit. I will stay a week."

"I am not in the habit of inviting strange knights to stay in my home."

"How's your head after that nasty knock you took, Nicolaus?"

Amsdorf's confusion melted into recognition. "Martin!" he whispered. "Come in."

Martin entered quickly. Melanchthon looked up from his morning bread. "Come, Nicolaus, who is your friend?"

Amsdorf paused for a moment and Martin answered instead. "Knight Jörg at your service, esteemed gentleman."

Melanchthon took in the knight before turning to Amsdorf. "I was not aware that you were friendly with knights." Both Martin and Amsdorf laughed heartily before Martin introduced himself once more with a more forthcoming attitude. Once he had recovered from his shock, Melanchthon had an idea. "Let's summon Lucas Cranach to paint the portrait of Knight Jörg! He has painted your picture before; perhaps he will know you after several hours of staring at your face!"

Several hours came and went, and Cranach, too, was shocked to discover the identity of Martin Luther. When the men informed Martin that Karlstadt had attacked the vows that forbid monks from taking wives, Martin gasped. "Good heavens! Will our Wittenbergers give wives even to monks? They won't force one on me!"[3]

Martin remained in Wittenberg a week before returning to the Wartburg, content with the progress being made to reform the church. He left Gabriel Zwilling, who was passionate about reform, in charge of preaching to the fifteen monks remaining at the Black Cloister. Martin felt confident that in spite of Andreas Karlstadt's rash behavior, the war with the dragon was moving forward, even without Martin present to fight it.

Once settled back in his little room at the Wartburg, safe from the threat of execution for heresy, Martin decided to translate the New Testament from Greek into a German dialect that every German could understand. He worked quickly, translating the Scriptures in just under three months. The task was difficult, and Martin struggled to combine the different forms of the German language into one dialect for everyone. Martin didn't know it, but as he was translating the Bible, he was also rewriting the German language.

Martin pushed aside his translation to write a letter to his dear friend and advisor, Georg Spalatin.

I have undertaken to translate the Bible into German. This was good for me; otherwise I might have died with the mistaken notion that I was a learned fellow.[4]

Martin thought with some satisfaction about his struggle with the devil. That terrible dragon had plagued him for many years.

See Spalatin, I have thrown ink at Satan.[5]

He believed that his new translation of God's Word— the Sword of the Spirit—would act as a sharp dagger thrust beneath the scales of the serpent, exposing the soft underbelly of his opponent.

━ ∎ ━

January and February of 1522 brought an increase in changes not only to Wittenberg, but to Germany as well.

Riots became more common, and mobs interrupted services, burning church statues and paintings in the belief they constituted outright idolatry, and removing the altars from churches. Karlstadt began to call himself "Brother Andreas." He wore the clothes of a commoner and married a fifteen-year-old girl. The Augustinians held a council and released the monks from their vows to pursue work in the cities and villages. Any monk who chose to remain in a monastery was now required to devote himself to preaching and serving in the community, rather than serving only his fellow monks or enriching his spiritual life in solitude.

Men calling themselves the Zwickau Prophets entered Wittenberg and began to preach that the end of the world was coming. From his room in the kingdom of the birds, Martin read of their arrival and while he agreed that the world would end soon, he was outraged to hear that the men were claiming that wisdom comes from the Holy Spirit alone rather than from Scripture. People in Wittenberg and the surrounding areas began to question the baptism of infants as a humanmade tradition rather than a scriptural one. Martin was incensed—everywhere men were making doctrinal decisions he did not agree with. In the midst of riots and new prophets, the Wittenberg city council wrote Martin a letter begging him to return home.

Early on the morning of March 2, 1522, thirty-eight-year-old Martin pulled on his wool tights, slung his crimson cloak over his shoulder, strapped on his sword, and set out for home.

Chapter 17

THE KNIGHT RETURNS

Spring 1522–Spring 1523

Friends, we cannot turn the hearts of unbelievers to Christ at the point of a sword." Martin grasped the side of the small rounded stone deck he stood upon in the Town Church and leaned forward with an intensity that radiated from his rounded face. In the audience were young women clutching babies, noblemen with long beards, ruddy-faced peasant farmers, and runaway nuns still wearing their white linen head coverings. Martin inhaled the familiar smell of sweat, manure, and hopeful expectations. The sullen faces of Andreas Karlstadt and Gabriel Zwilling, the new preacher Martin had installed, glared at him from the back. Karlstadt had become increasingly radical, but

Zwilling was ready to incite war in the name of reforming the church. "We do not win the unbelieving to Christ as the Romans won Germany."

Martin shook his head. "A faith without love is not enough. Indeed, it is no faith at all; in fact, it is a false faith, just as a face seen in a mirror is not a face but merely the image of one."[1]

He closed his eyes and envisioned the riots that had been taking place. Altars and paintings were smashed and priests had been run off. He thought of that terrible torture device that smashed the thumbs, screwing two metal bars closer and closer together until a man would do anything to avoid the pain. His eyes snapped open. He looked directly at Karlstadt and Zwilling and pointed. "No foe, regardless of how much pain he has inflicted against me, has put the screws to me as you have right here. You, sirs, are in grave error."[2]

For eight long days, Martin preached against the fanatic and urgent push to transform the church without regard for the hearts of people. He urged people to slow down, to love their neighbors, to allow God to work in his own time.

"Excuse me, Doctor Luther? I wonder if you might have a moment?" Martin turned to see an elegant Italian man standing before him.

"Are you here as a representative of the church?" Martin could not believe the papacy had located him so quickly after his return.

The man colored slightly. "I am. My name is Fabricius Capito." Capito's square face and deep-set eyes were framed by a carefully trimmed beard. "I come as a representative of

Albert of Mainz. Could I have a few moments of your time, please? I have some questions about this love you speak of."

Martin examined the man for a moment before leading him to his study for a long and fruitful conversation. Capito left Wittenberg with a newly printed copy of Martin's translation of the New Testament—and with a new heart.

▬ ▬ ▬

Martin was praying beneath the pear tree outside the Black Cloister one morning when Melanchthon approached with a portly man dressed in a black scholar's gown. His nose was straight with a crook near the middle indicating it may once have been broken. His full cheeks extended into the space between his chin and his neck. Absent-mindedly, Martin felt his own smooth face. Though he'd shaved the beard, his hair remained long; never again would he wear a tonsure. Martin noticed that his cheeks also had begun to descend lower, giving him a fold of padded skin just beneath his chin. His neck rose to meet his new jowls in greeting. He patted his stomach. *I suppose I had my fill of good food at the Wartburg.*

"Martin, I would like you to meet Johannes Bugenhagen. He arrived in your absence and is an expert in the ancient languages."

Martin glanced at Melanchthon. "Well, if you are willing to declare him an expert, my Greek grammarian, it must be so." He turned to Bugenhagen with a nod. "And tell me, sir, how do you find my teachings? I have seen you seated in the church this week."

Bugenhagen cleared his throat. "I have read your newly printed German New Testament, and I find your work with the German language extraordinary. Of course, there are things you could improve in your translation of the Greek."

"And my teachings?"

The professor stared past Martin for a moment before answering. "I must admit that when I read a copy of *On the Babylonian Captivity of the Church*, I thought you the king of all heretics."

Martin frowned. *Are you alone wise?* played through his mind again and from habit he listened for the drumbeat of distant wings whirring toward him. "And now? Am I a heretic still?"

Bugenhagen laughed. "Now I say to myself, 'The entire world is blind, for this man is the only one who sees the truth.'[3] I have been converted, Doctor Luther, and I will help you with your Bible translation, and I will travel the countryside to help spread your New Theology. I have plans also to visit the king of Denmark. He has heard this gospel and is eager to learn more."

Martin's mouth opened slightly. The dragon retreated and instead Martin felt certain the sound of an angel chorus echoed through his heart. For the rest of his days, Martin would seek Bugenhagen each day to confess his sins.

— ■ —

"Leonhard! How are you, my friend? What is the news?" Martin embraced the merchant who supplied the Black Cloister with beer and herring. Leonhard Koppe made a good living traveling throughout a wide region with his wares. "You smell like Jonah after three days within the belly of the great fish!"

Koppe laughed. "I can no longer smell fish—or much at all for that matter! As for the news, I bring you good tidings."

In the spring of 1523, thirty-nine-year-old Martin had been home in Wittenberg for a little over a year, and things had changed. Andreas Karlstadt and Gabriel Zwilling had left town. The Zwickau Prophets no longer preached their mystical message from the streets of Wittenberg. In the place of the radical pastors, nuns running from their convents began appearing in the city like disoriented birds who had lost their way during a migration south. Martin did his best to help each one find a husband or work in a nearby town. After declaring that nuns and priests should marry, he felt responsible for their welfare. Many of the women had been pledged to the convents as small children with no freedom to choose their own future.

Koppe sat on the end of his wagon, nestling between two wooden barrels of beer. "The reformation spreads, even as you and I exchange news. Across Germany, pastors are taking the place of priests." The merchant counted across his fingertips. "In Strasbourg, Martin Bucer joins Fabricius Capito in solidifying the New Theology."

Martin laughed. "Capito? Why, he was a representative of that wolf, Albert the Archbishop of Mainz! And Bucer I met five years ago in Heidelberg where I was relieved of my duties to the Augustinian order."

"Your teachings have had quite an impact!"

Martin shook his head. "The message of the cross has had the impact. God's Word never returns void."

Koppe nodded in agreement. "In Basel, Johannes Oecolampadius is doing well to spread the true message of the cross. And in Switzerland, the pastor Ulrich Zwingli reports that his people are well fed on milk and will soon be ready for solid food."

Martin smiled at that reference to Scripture. "I am happy to say that Johannes Bugenhagen has been traveling through Germany on occasion and has even been to Denmark. The reformation is spreading, and Scripture is ringing true for many. It is unfortunate that many still try to force the reformation of the church to move faster than God would have it occur. I fear that Karlstadt, Zwilling, and the 'prophets' will push us to war."

A group of young women passed Martin and Koppe while they chatted on College Street. The women wore black gowns, but their hair flowed free. They laughed and waved to Martin as they passed. Koppe watched with a puzzled expression. "More nuns? It seems you are overrun with them these days. So tell me, Doctor, of the news here in Wittenberg."

Martin sighed. "It is true that we have more than our fair share of escaped nuns. It seems that every time I manage to find one of them a permanent position—or a marriage— more arrive. Their stories are hard. Sold or given to the convents at such young ages, and compelled by the laws of Rome to remain imprisoned there." The monk shifted uneasily. "Leonhard. I know how you desire to help the

Reformation spread. How could a warrior possibly do more damage to the old dragon Satan than by enabling healthy families to preach the Word of God in their own homes?"

Koppe tilted his head. "You seem to have a request, Doctor. How can I help?"

"I have received a letter from a . . . ," Martin pulled a wad of paper from within his gown and flipped to the end. "A Katharina von Bora. She is one of twelve nuns from a convent in Targau. They wish to flee, Leonhard."

"But that is Duke George's territory, Doctor."

"Yes."

"Prince Frederick pretends not to see the nuns, but Duke George—the penalty for fleeing a convent is death."

"As is the penalty for helping nuns escape."

The men were silent. Leonhard Koppe examined a splinter jutting from the wooden side of his cart while Martin folded the letter and placed it back into his gown. Finally, Leonhard unloaded barrels of herring from his wagon before retrieving the empty kegs the monks had set on the porch of the Black Cloister.

The sixty-year-old-man straightened his collar and leveled his gaze with Martin's. "I have delivered your goods, Doctor. I plan to be by again shortly after the eve of the resurrection. I will be coming from Duke George's territory in the vicinity of Targau. Do you remember that story you preached from the pulpit of the Town Church? About the maidens who await the bridegroom? The ones who are prepared with oil in their lamps are ushered into the wedding feast." The old merchant took a deep breath, inflating his chest. He exhaled with purpose, narrowing his eyes. "See that you preach that story, Doctor. The maidens must be ready for the feast."

Martin grinned. "I will preach it, you old fox."

— — —

It was a joyful service that Martin preached Saturday evening before the celebration of Christ's resurrection. He was traveling from the Town Church to the Black Cloister when a group of students ran past him. "Doctor!" panted one. "A wagon load of maidens has just come to town, all more eager for marriage than for life." He laughed. "God grant them husbands lest worse befall them."[4]

Martin hurried home, muttering, "God grant them husbands indeed."

Martin turned through the yard leading to the cloister, but gasped when he saw the wagon. Leonhard was helping the last of nine women out of a herring barrel. The smell of sour fish made Martin's knees buckle. But it was the appearance of the women that truly shocked him. Each was dressed in the full garb of a nun, smeared with noxious oily fish scales and innards.

"Leonhard, you could not have found another manner in which to transport them? The stench is unbearable."

The merchant glared at Martin. "You ordered twelve nuns. I have delivered three to their homes, and brought you the remaining nine. I should think a little fish smell a small price to pay to retain my head."

A woman in her early twenties hopped off the cart and strode over to Martin. Her wide-set eyes took him in. "So you are the famous Doctor? I must say, you are plumper than I imagined. I admire your work greatly, and thank you for the rescue. If you think our odor is bad, you should try riding in one of the barrels yourself." With that, the lady turned and entered the Black Cloister, beckoning her friends to follow.

Martin stood below the former monastery fingering his growing jowls.

Chapter 18

WAR AND A WEDDING

Spring 1523–July 1525

icolaus von Amsdorf handed Philipp Melanchthon and Martin Luther steel mugs. "Have a seat, friends. Tell us, Martin, how goes the search for homes for the remaining nuns?"

Martin sat with a heavy sigh. "I have written letters, and all but begged. I have but one nun left who is without a home, Katharina von Bora, the one everyone calls Katie. She was engaged to a student to be married, but he has taken leave of the city, and has not responded to my attempts to reach him. I believe he's abandoned her. I am at a loss. The woman is twenty-five years old. She is past the age of marriage and she is . . ."

Melanchthon laughed. "Opinionated."

"Yes. That is a kind way to put it. Other words come
to my mind. Someone actually suggested I marry Katie."
Martin chuckled before growing serious. "I am not now
inclined to take a wife. Not that I lack the feelings of a man,
for I am neither wood nor stone, but my mind is averse
to marriage because I daily expect the death decreed to
the heretic.[1] A woman—even an old, opinionated nun—
deserves a husband who will live out the year."

Amsdorf frowned. "It has been a year since the first
martyrs of our cause were burned in the Netherlands.
However, that man Thomas Müntzer is doing his best to
cause the deaths of many. Setting fire to the chapel outside
Alstedt was, I fear, the first of his poor choices. I hear he has
gathered to him a small army of two thousand men in Alstedt. He claims all his teachings come to him in dreams."

Martin stood to his feet in anger. "These Alstedters
revile the Bible and rave about the Spirit, but where do
they show the fruits of the Spirit, love, joy, peace, and
patience?" Martin spat his words. He could feel the heat
rising from his chest into his face. Resentment and anger
were not new emotions for Martin, but lately they over-
whelmed him at every turn. "I must write a letter to the
princes. They must banish the offenders from the land. The
office of pastor is simply preaching and suffering. Christ
and the apostles did not smash images and churches, but
rather won hearts with God's Word." He paced the floor,
working into his next statement. His breath felt hot and
ragged, as if the priest himself could breathe fire. "If these

Alstedters want to wipe out the ungodly, they will have to bathe in blood!"[2]

Melanchthon gasped. "Martin, your anger! You have spoken to me of fighting a great dragon, but it seems now you direct your battle at any foe—or friend—in your path. We fought Rome when I wished to reconcile. Must we now fight fellow pastors, no matter how misguided they may be? Anger is a sin, do you recall?"

Martin turned on Melanchthon. "Anger refreshes all my blood, sharpens my mind, and drives away temptations.[3] And now that we have won such a great battle over the Word of God, I will not sacrifice the details."

Amsdorf urged Martin to sit. "Come, Martin, tell us about your hymns."

Martin struggled to regain himself. "Well, as you know, I wrote my first hymn last year about our two martyrs." Amsdorf and Melanchthon nodded. "Yet, I'm just now getting the hang of it. It's nearing the end of the year. I hope to have at least twenty hymns written by the time we reach 1525 in a month or so."

Melanchthon looked surprised. "Twenty?"

"Yes, Philipp. With the chaos occurring in every congregation across Germany, we need an effective way to bring order to the services. There also seems to be no better way to teach theology than through song."

"Well, the services certainly are chaotic," said Melanchthon, nodding in agreement. "Last week, I heard of a priest who was conducting Reformed services in the morning and Mass in the afternoon."

Amsdorf frowned. "That's actually not uncommon. We're headed for a storm, friends."

Martin and his friends had no way of knowing that already the storm had begun. In August, deep in the Black Forest of the Rhine Valley, the countess of Lüpfen had demanded that the peasants gather strawberries and snail shells for a banquet she was throwing, although it was a church holiday. Outraged, the peasants refused. News of their rebellion spread, and large gatherings of angry peasants began to march through the countryside in search of support.

━ ■ ━

It was during the spring of 1525 that Martin abandoned all hope of marrying Katharina von Bora to the student who had broken off their engagement without a word of explanation. Instead, Martin sent his friend Nicolaus von Amsdorf to inform Katie she could marry the older—and somewhat grumpy—Kaspar Glatz. With that responsibility handled, Martin turned his attention to more pressing, and more violent, matters.

Melanchthon knocked on the frame of Martin's open door to his tower office. His thin, delicate face looked haggard. Martin set down his quill pen, beckoned his friend enter, and paced the room. "What am I supposed to do? I have read the declaration written by the peasant leaders, *The Twelve Articles of the Swabian Peasants*. I have visited their camps and worked to solve the issue. I have even written *An Admonition to Peace*, in which I stated that the lords and princes demand too much—that they are responsible for this rebellion. I have reminded the peasants that they are to submit, that they must not ever appeal to the gospel as a reason for their violence. Yet, despite all my selfless work to end this uprising, even now, the poor are sacking castles and cloisters. Cloisters, Philipp! They are harming monks."

Martin turned to Melanchthon. He could feel his face growing red and his stomach twisting. Melanchthon softly groaned. "Martin, I beg of you to mediate this issue. This could quickly become a full-fledged war, and many lives could be lost. The peasants had a number of good points written in *The Twelve Articles*. They should be able to hunt and gather wood. Their cattle should be allowed to graze in the meadows. I beg of you, Martin—deal softly with this issue. The peasants have called you as their mediator. Make peace on all sides."

Martin began to pace. The peasants did have some reasonable demands, but many of their requirements involved the church. Martin felt the peasants had no right to issue ultimatums about how the church should be run. Again, he felt a fire in his bones, and the rough breath of an anger that heated his soul and warmed his body through.

"It's not right that these peasants are killing our leadership!" The monk punched the air for emphasis. "And that man Müntzer is involved, leading them to murder and pillage! He claims his dreams are from God—that God tells him his sleeves will catch all bullets. The man is a false prophet and a false general." Martin spun around stabbing an invisible foe. "Devils and dragons! The peasants have all been possessed by demons. The only way to deal with a dragon is to slay it." Martin narrowed his gaze at his peace-making friend. "Get out, Philipp! Peace can only reach so far. I have work to do."

Melanchthon left with a look of dread upon his face.

Martin picked up his quill and a new sheet of paper. Across the top of the page, he scrawled "Against the Murderous and Thieving Hordes of Peasants." Martin's anger and dismay at the dragons that once roamed the air and now inhabited the people of his land poured onto the page like hot copper pouring from a smelting pot into the mold. Martin would mold his Germany.

> *Every man is at once judge and executioner of a public rebel; just as, when a fire starts, he who can extinguish it first is the best fellow. Rebellion is not simply vile murder, but is like a great fire that kindles and devastates a country; it fills the land with murder and bloodshed, makes widows and orphans, and destroys everything, like the greatest calamity.*[4]

The irate priest's eyes narrowed as he thought of the many hundreds of castles and monasteries that lay in ruins across Germany due to the violent uprising that was occurring. He shook his head in dismay over the noble families that were murdered, children and all. Something must be done, and he was the one to do it.

> *Therefore, whosoever can, should smite, strangle, and stab, secretly or publicly, and should remember that there is nothing more poisonous, pernicious, and devilish than a rebellious man. Just as one must slay a mad dog, so, if you do not fight the rebels, they will fight you, and the whole country with you.*[5]

Martin lay down his quill, forgetting that he, too, was a true rebel. He would finish his letter and take it to the printer that day.

Throughout Germany, the princes had already begun to take action. They had called out their knights and saddled their horses, ready to bear down on the farmers armed with pitchforks and sharpened sticks. Thomas Müntzer was preparing his army of five thousand to march. He would soon discover that his sleeves were not magic, nor could they catch bullets.

___ ■ ___

Martin saw Amsdorf coming across the university campus long before they were within speaking range. The look on his long face was foreboding. "Martin, Katie will not marry Kaspar Glatz. She says she will only marry me—or you, Martin."

Martin froze. "What? Oh, my friend, you jest!" Martin slapped Amsdorf on the back.

Amsdorf tipped his head to the side. "No, friend, I never jest about marriage. And I must say, I have no intention of marrying Katharina von Bora." With that, the professor spun on his heel and walked away.

Martin spent the month of May considering a marriage to Katie. He did not love her, that was certain, but when Martin jokingly mentioned the possibility of a marital union to his father on a trip home, Hans was greatly excited by the prospect of the marriage. In fact, Hans was excited about all of the changes his son was creating in Germany.

Martin decided that marriage was perhaps the best way to show how serious he was about abandoning church traditions and living according to the Word of God. Also, marrying opinionated, twenty-six-year-old Katie would solve the dilemma of what to do with her.

It was a sunny day in the middle of June when Martin approached Katie. She looked up at him with a questioning glance, her small lips pursing over her diminutive, pointed chin. "Katie! I have decided that we should be wed. If it is true that you will have a portly forty-three-year-old monk for a husband, I should marry you to gratify my father and to spite the Devil."[6]

Katie wrinkled her straight nose at him. "Well, don't forget that you shall marry me because I keep a good garden and shall make you the best beer in all of Germany."

Martin laughed heartily. "Those, too, are good reasons. We shall have our wedding celebration in two weeks. I shall invite my parents, Georg Spalatin and Nicolaus von Amsdorf, and of course that herring dealer Leonhard Koppe."

Katie frowned. "I will never eat another herring for as long as I live. The stench haunts me even in my dreams. We will ask the prince for the use of the Black Cloister. You and the prior are the only ones living there now, and with a little work I can turn it into an inn and a place for you to meet with your students. You will not regret my cooking." Her blue eyes sparkled beneath her chestnut hair, which was woven into a simple bun. "Over there, past your pear tree, we shall have a lovely garden."

On the morning of the twenty-seventh of June, 1525, Martin escorted Katie down College Street to the sound of pealing church bells. At the Town Church, they were married in the doorway, with the people of Wittenberg standing in the market square. Only Philipp Melanchthon was missing. After their disagreement regarding the peasant uprising, Martin had chosen not to invite his close friend.

For lunch, the new couple held a banquet in the hall of the Black Cloister. There was a lively dance before the party settled down for a second feast. Gifts were piled high along the walls, and laughter rang through the empty cells of the monastery.

Katie and Martin joyously embraced each of their guests as they left for the evening. Martin swung the heavy door shut and turned to his bride. "We have done it, Katie! We have wed—the monk and the nun are married!"

Katie smiled and opened her mouth to reply, but was distracted by a frantic pounding on the door behind them. "Why it's eleven o'clock at night, and on our wedding night, no less. Who could that possibly be?"

Martin swung the door wide to find Andreas Karlstadt, disheveled and sweating. "Martin, I need shelter. The people have lost their minds. My reforms have gone awry, and I am pursued."

Martin turned to his nun and sighed. "Katie, on our wedding night, I will need you to make up another bed for our guest."

Katie smiled and swayed down the hall. This guest would be the first of many, and the halls of the Black Cloister would never again be silent or still.

Chapter 19

OUR GOD REIGNS

July 1525–December 1527

Katie!" Martin stomped past the little vegetable garden he tended each morning. Rows of peas, melons, and cucumbers smiled up at him in the late summer sunshine. The pastor headed for the orchard where Katie often tended to the apple and nut trees. "Kaaatieee!" Martin's voice was hoarse from calling. He had already spent several minutes searching the massive Black Cloister for his wife.

Martin reversed course and headed for the fish pond. There, on the bank of the water, Katie was straddling several large rocks and swinging a net through the pond. Her pigtails bobbed beneath her bonnet, and the tip of her tongue was plastered to her upper lip in concentration. Martin watched as she pulled out a large, wriggling carp. In triumph, she tossed it against the grass where it flopped around with several others. Martin took the opportunity to get her attention. "Excuse me, my lord, but I wonder if you have seen the vase I mean to send to Georg Spalatin as a wedding gift. It seems to have grown legs and wandered off."

Katie leaned against the pole of her fishing net. "Do you mean the vase that we received as a wedding gift? If that is the one you are thinking of, Doctor, I shouldn't wonder that you cannot find it. You see, I have hidden it."

Martin's eyes widened in anger. "First, you cry like—like a woman, and I must stay home from the wedding of my dear friend. Now, you hide my gift to him? The gift given to me by my friends?" At this point, Martin was roaring.

Katie looked skyward. "The gift given to *us*. We will sell the vase this winter for grain. If you should stop giving away everything we own, I would not have to hide the valuables to pay the bills. As for the wedding, Doctor, there was a war occurring. You cannot travel to a wedding when you may be killed on the side of the road. You have placed me in charge of the accounts, and I shall do my best to keep them up to date." Katie returned to the pond with her net. By now, the fish on the grass were still.

"If I should ever marry again, I would hew myself an obedient wife out of stone![1] If I can survive the wrath of the Devil in my sinful conscience, I can withstand the anger of Katharina von Bora!"[2] Martin stormed back to the Black Cloister and up to the study. He read the last line of his letter. "*I am sending you a vase as a present.*" He dipped his quill in the ink and wrote, "*P.S. Katie's hidden it.*"[3]

"Doctor, could you tell us about your book *On the Bondage of the Will* that you published last month? Was your response aimed directly at Erasmus's book *A Diatribe on the Freedom of the Will*? Why did you wait more than a year after it was written to respond?"

It was January of 1526. Martin looked down his large dining-room table at the nearly thirty students who came to dinner that night in the Black Cloister. His eyes rested on Melanchthon, who raised an eyebrow at him. Martin remembered the many discussions in which his good friend begged him to remain at peace with Erasmus, the scholar from the Netherlands.

"Why did I remain so long silent? Well, I cannot describe how terrible I felt about that little book by Erasmus on the freedom of the will. It is very difficult for me to answer such an unlearned book from such a learned man."[4]

A student at the end of the table opened a little book. "My favorite part of the book, Doctor Luther, and the part that helped me understand your point is where you write that the human will is like a beast between God and Satan." He cleared his throat and began to read. " 'If God mounts it, it wishes and goes as God wills. . . . If Satan mounts it, it wishes and goes as Satan wills. Nor can it choose the rider it would prefer, nor betake itself to him, but it is the riders who contend for its possession.'[5] It sounds as if we must hope and pray we are the beast chosen and won by God."

Martin had leaned back in his chair and closed his eyes in order to concentrate on his own words. Katie entered the room with another tray of bread and a platter of pork she had slaughtered herself that morning. Her stomach was just barely beginning to protrude under the folds of her smock, but she walked carefully as women do when they are avoiding the scent of the dishes they carry during pregnancy.

"Perhaps we should hear what Frau Luther has to say on the issue," suggested a red-haired young man down the table from the renowned professor.

Martin's eyes snapped open. "It is important to consider the advice of those who have actually battled with Satan himself. Those who have walked through the long dark night of the soul, and have gone to war with the dragon, like myself." Martin heard Katie huff softly. He thought it best to avoid her wrath. "Though, I must say, I am an inferior lord. Katie is superior. I am Aaron, she is Moses."[6] Martin smiled sweetly at his wife. *That ought to help calm her spirits.*

Katie's eyes narrowed. Setting the trays down on the table, she swiveled and walked briskly away. "Katie! Are you not planning to serve us?" Martin called after his wife. There was no response but the receding click of Katie's heels down the hall. Martin sighed. "Impossible nun. She does as she pleases. Ludwig, would you please serve the pork?"

Ludwig stood and began to walk the tray around the table, offering a slice to each visitor. "I understand that you are involved in a discussion with Ulrich Zwingli, Johannes Oecolampadius, Martin Bucer, and Fabricius Capito over the true meaning of the Lord's Supper, Doctor Luther."

Martin sniffed. "It is ridiculous to think that Christ meant 'This is my body' as only a symbol. That view would seem to weaken all Scripture. One cannot alter the words of Scripture with human reason."

A bearded visitor spoke up. "Even if human reason would indicate that Christ actually did mean 'This is my body' symbolically? I am not a doctor of theology, but the bread and the wine still appear to be bread and wine, not blood or a piece of flesh."

Martin could feel the burn beginning in his chest. *How dare a visitor to my table . . .*

At that moment, Katie returned, a hand on her bulging belly and one across her brow. "Doctor. I have fainted in my room. I have done battle with Satan, just as you have. I am quite certain it is the first of many times to come." She closed her eyes in exhaustion.

Martin forgot his ire, and rose to greet his triumphant wife. *She too has battled the dragon! Oh, what a wife the Lord has given me!*

Melanchthon turned his head and coughed in an odd way that sounded nearly like a chuckle. "My Kette!" Martin used the German word for "chain" in a play on the name Katie. "I should have suspected you were strong enough to do so. The dragon is no match for the dear rib of Doctor Luther."

Katie opened one eye and peered sideways at Martin. "May I now participate in your discussion?"

Martin shoved his own chair to the side. "Ludwig! Bring my wife a chair."

— — —

Deep into the summer of 1527, Martin stumbled to the room he shared with Katie and collapsed across the bed. He'd been having dizzy spells since April and had even stopped preaching for a time. The month before, Martin had felt terrible, announcing it was his last night to live and calling his friends and Katie to his side.

Lying down will make the room still again, thought Martin. He closed his eyes, willing the lurching in his stomach to pass. Nearby, a fly tormented the left side of his head. The buzzing increased, whirring and humming, until Martin was certain a minuscule dragon had landed in his ear. He felt the warmth leave his hands and feet first. Soon, his entire body felt near frozen as heat fled from him. Martin shook uncontrollably, clawing at his left ear, where the buzzing continued.

"Katie! Kaaatiiee! Bring me water! Do you hear me Katie? I am going to die!"

Far away, from the kitchen of the Black Cloister, Martin could hear stoneware drop and the urgent pounding of his wife's feet against the cold wooden floor. He sank into blackness.

━ ∎ ━

"I think you will recover, Doctor Luther, though you may never fully regain your strength." The physician gazed grimly at his patient. "Then again, you have not been in good health for quite some time. I advise you to work less, Doctor. Preaching eight times a week is too much."

Martin scoffed aloud. From his sickbed, it sounded more like a whimper. The doctor set his mouth and stared at the wall. "Doctor Luther, you should leave Wittenberg with your wife and child now. I saw the first signs of plague early this morning, and I can tell you we will all be fortunate if we survive. You are already weakened, and will surely never live through the coming onslaught."

Martin's tired brain worked hard to process this new piece of information. From the corner of his eye, he spotted Katie moving behind the doctor with a pitcher of water. Little Hans had his feet planted widely on the floor and was attempting to push himself upward with his hands. He stood for a moment, wobbled, and sat down hard at his mother's feet.

Katie walked to Martin's side with a mug of water. "Thank you, sir. We will not be leaving, will we, Martin?" She laughed. "Can you imagine a monk and a nun fleeing in the moment of need, when people will be most able to hear the truth of the gospel?"

The doctor looked at Katie in horror. "Frau Luther. You are clearly pregnant—again. And you have a son to care for."

Martin struggled to sit in his bed. "Katie is right. We may fear greatly, but we will not flee. We will turn the Black Cloister into a hospital, so that ordinary citizens will not be forced to do so with their homes."

The doctor glared at Martin. "Well, I will not stay to bury you or the rest of Wittenberg. My cart and my family are waiting for me on College Street. I leave you to your fate."

Martin and Katie did stay. The Black Cloister soon held the sick and the dying from across Wittenberg. The former monastery was under quarantine, and the only visitor was the daily cart that picked up the bodies of the dead.

Martin suffered again with his strange buzzing illness, but Katie soldiered on, caring for all beneath her roof. It was a cold fall day when Martin emerged from his study, shaken and exhausted from the effort required to remain upright, to find that not one of their patients had been fed. Hans sat on the floor outside the bedroom his parents shared and cried pitifully.

Martin scooped up his boy and rushed into the room. The dank stench of death hit him like a club before he saw Katie. She was lying on the floor, one arm stretched out underneath her. Her eyes rolled slowly up to see Martin and her son. The sick woman's belly rose far into the air, a reminder of the life within her.

"Oh Katie! Do not die and leave me!"[7] Martin sank to the ground beside the nun he had grown to dearly love. He choked. The skin on Katie's cheek was so hot it nearly burnt his hand.

"Katie," Martin stumbled through his tears. Hans stroked his mother's hair. "Katie, I have written a hymn. I will sing it for you." Martin's clear, high voice was deepened and gravelly with emotion.

> A mighty fortress is our God,
> A bulwark never failing;
> Our helper He, amid the flood
> Of mortal ills prevailing;
> For still our ancient foe
> Doth seek to work us woe;
> His craft and power are great,
> And, armed with cruel hate,
> On Earth is not his equal.

Did we in our own strength confide,
Our striving would be losing;
Were not the right Man on our side,
The Man of God's own choosing;
Dost ask who that may be?
Christ Jesus, it is He;
Lord Sabaoth, His name,
From age to age the same,
And He must win the battle.

And though this world, with devils filled,
Should threaten to undo us,
We will not fear, for God hath willed
His truth to triumph through us.
The Prince of Darkness grim—
We tremble not for him;
His rage we can endure,
For lo, his doom is sure,
One little word shall fell him.

That word above all earthly powers,
No thanks to them, abideth.
The Spirit and the gift are ours
Through Him who with us sideth;
Let goods and kindred go,
This mortal life also;
The body they may kill;
God's truth abideth still,
His kingdom is forever.[8]

Martin sobbed and clutched Katie's hand. "Oh, Katie.
I know where you are headed. But don't go there yet."

Chapter 20

BUT WHAT SHALL WE TEACH?

December 1527–1529

Martin fingered a fat gold ring before examining the others upon his round fingers. The voluminous satin sleeves of his high-necked black jacket draped down his arms, setting the rings off perfectly. His nobleman's leggings were snug against his legs. Over the back of his chair, Martin had draped his black coat, the fox-fur lining shining in the light. His favorite large pendant hung heavy down his wide chest. Freshly shaved after his weekly bath, forty-five-year-old Martin felt ready for his preaching that evening. He noted with pride that the students at his heavy wooden table had come prepared with their notebooks and quills. Martin thrived on the scratching of their pens as he spoke. Certainly, not many former monks had scribes to record their every word.

A peal of laughter from down the table shook Martin from his thoughts. *Not many former monks likely oversee a household full of children, either.* Martin and Katie were gradually adding to their household—a nephew here and two nieces and four nephews there. Aunt Lena sat at the table with little Hans, who would be three in a month, and helped him choose food from the center. Martin remembered the day Aunt Lena had climbed out of a herring barrel alongside her niece, Katie.

Just then Katie bustled into the room, her enormous belly preceding her entrance by more than a foot. She wore the high-necked dress of a noblewoman with a tailored black jacket over the top and a soft peach scarf wound around her neck and over her head. Her dress had not been cinched down over the ribs or waist in months to make room for the new baby.

"Ah, there is the priestess of Wittenberg, my Kette." Martin smiled at his bride. Katie smiled back and began to fill mugs with her famous homemade brew. "Katie, I am telling our guests of the schools we must form."

Martin turned to speak down the center of the large ornate table in the dining hall. "The Scripture cannot be understood without the languages, and the languages can be learned only in school."[1]

A bearded student interrupted. "Doctor, many families depend on their children to help with the harvest."

Martin nodded. "If parents cannot spare their children for a full day, let them send them for a part. I would wager that in half of Germany there are not over four thousand pupils in school." He snorted, his neck growing ruddy with emotion. "I would like to know where we are going to get our pastors and teachers three years from now."[2]

Hans looked up at Katie and did his best to snort like his father. She rolled her eyes.

Martin picked up a small bound book and waved it. "Alas, what manifold misery I beheld! The common people, especially in the villages, know nothing at all of Christian doctrine."[3] The reformer snorted again. Down the table, a small snort echoed. "And many pastors are quite unfit and incompetent to teach. Yet all are called Christians, are baptized, and enjoy the use of the sacraments, although they know neither the Lord's Prayer, the Apostles' Creed, nor the Ten Commandments!"[4]

Martin stood and pounded the table with his fist. He felt the rush of heat into his face, and his stomach churned. "They live like the poor brutes and irrational swine. Still they have, now that the gospel has come, learned to abuse all liberty in a masterly manner!"[5] Martin ended his speech by punching the air with a pointed finger. Down the table, a little arm waved in the air, just as his father's had.

One of the bolder students pointed to the book Martin held in his other hand. "Doctor, what is it that you have written?" Martin smiled. "It is *The Small Catechism*. It is the duty of every father to question and examine his children and servants at least once a week, and until they repeat what they have learned of what every Christian must know, they should be given neither food nor drink!"[6] A stabbing pain shot from Martin's belly into his chest and he sat abruptly.

"Will you use *The Small Catechism* with your family?" The student at the end of the table wore his hair short and his face was beardless.

Martin nodded. "Aunt Lena, Hans, my Lutheress, and the little one she carries shall all learn every evening. We shall end by singing a hymn. The common people learn true theology through music, you know. That is why the congregations in Germany now sing." The professor's eyes watered and his vision blurred. "Had little Elizabeth survived more than a few months, I would have helped her as well." He looked across the room to Katie who was carrying a fresh tray of bread to the table. "That was a terrible plague, wasn't it, Katie?"

Katie opened her mouth to respond, but instead dropped the tray and gripped the sideboard, moaning loudly. Slices of bread bounced across the floor. Martin sprang to his feet. "And here comes another small Luther. To bed with you, my little lord and master."

━━ ▪ ━━

Martin Luther and Philipp Melanchthon stood at the base of the hill, gazing through the trees upon the sprawling giant of the Marburg Castle.

"I tell you, Philipp, no good will come of this meeting."

Melanchthon stroked the thin beard on his sculpted chin as the two men huffed their way toward the stone building. "It can't go well. After all, the Protestants are opposed to the truth of the Eucharist. And you did call Ulrich Zwingli a tool of Satan."

Martin grunted loudly and wrapped his arms around his sore belly. "These princes who protested against Ferdinand have courage. Protestants—as they call themselves— have adopted my idea that the church must be reformed by the governors and princes of this world. Yet, Philip of Hesse should stay out of doctrinal affairs. This is the fight of priests and monks. He is a young and restless prince[7] who should not be heeded. Yet, I have agreed to meet with the Sacramentarians only because of my respect for Prince John of our beloved Saxony and his brother Frederick the Wise, God rest his soul."

Melanchthon looked askance at Martin. "There is no other reason we meet today?"

"God willing, I will not have it that our opponents may boast that they were more inclined to peace and unity than I was."[8]

Melanchthon squinted up at the hulking castle before fixing his gaze on Martin. "The situation is strange, friend. So much has happened this past year. Have you heard? Ferdinand, that rapscallion of a brother of Emperor Charles V, has blamed you for the Turks attacking."

Martin laughed loudly. "Yes, and I answered him boldly with my book *Concerning War against the Turks*! It should be clear to all true Christians that any crusade cannot be a holy war, justified by God. After all, the prince is not the head of Christendom. He cannot defend the true church."

Melanchthon was quiet for a moment. "Who is the head of Christendom, Martin? You? The pope? This reformation was never supposed to be about separating with our Christian brothers. I think we must enter the meeting today with a goal in mind. These men are not our enemies. Neither are they friends of the Church of Rome. Perhaps we can yet find unity among all. You could attempt to forgo an outburst." Melanchthon dropped back half a step and looked askance as if expecting a blow from his dear friend.

Martin felt the boil of his blood reach his chest before he heard the clear flute of his voice cross the hillside. "It is precisely because of my outbursts that the Lord has used me! I never work better than when I am inspired by anger; for when I am angry, I can write, pray, and preach well, for then my whole temperament is quickened, my understanding sharpened, and all mundane vexations and temptations depart."[9]

Melanchthon sighed. "Yes, but Martin, at some point we must stop fighting amongst ourselves and slay the dragon."

"Who is the dragon, Philipp?" Martin thundered in disdain. "There are so many dragons. They come from all sides and we must never rest. These men," he gestured toward the castle, "they fancy themselves leaders. But they twist the Word of God. And the Anabaptists—they, too, continue to be a thorn in my side. It is not just the view of baptism they hold to that concerns me, but their idea that the Holy Spirit gives private revelations to all men. They have taken my teaching of the priesthood of all believers and perverted it. They allow all men to preach whatever they so choose, untethered from Scripture. I will write about it!" Martin punched the air and felt a shock of pain run down his arm, through his heart, and into his gut. A wave of nausea washed over him and he grunted loudly.

"But Martin, this anger is not godly. The fruit of the Spirit . . ."

Martin felt the heat of rage surge into his veins like a lightning strike through the limbs of a branching tree. His passion was ignited in a flaming fury. "I was born to war with fanatics and devils. Thus my books are very stormy and bellicose. I must root out the stumps and trunks, hew away the thorns and briar, fill in the puddles. I am the rough woodsman, who must pioneer and hew a path."[10] He finished his speech with a flourish like a knight flashing his sword before an encroaching army. Martin had no doubt that God chose him to fight—and fight he would.

Melanchthon coughed awkwardly and nodded toward the landgrave of the castle who was rapidly moving toward the two men.

"Martin! I knew you would come! Enter my humble abode. The others are already present. Have you met my rotund wife, Christine? Look at how large she has grown in her second pregnancy. She may well have swallowed our entire melon patch!" Landgrave Philip of Hesse roared with laughter. His embroidered golden tunic rustled in the breeze beneath his rich satin jacket. Christine colored slightly, attempting to hide her belly behind Philip's massive costume.

Martin nodded to Christine with some compassion for her vulnerable state before fixing Philip with a contemptuous stare. "We've come. Let us proceed."

In the great hall of the castle of Marburg, Ulrich Zwingli shuffled forward, tears in his eyes. His plain black Swiss cap highlighted the absurdity of the oversized satin beret Philip of Hesse wore thrown up on one side, like a cat stretching its rump in the sun. "Doctors Luther and

Melanchthon. How very good to see you," Zwingli sniffed. "It is my hope—and the hope of Oecolampadius, Bucer, Capito, and the other guests—that we may be able to reach unity among the Protestant preachers. We sincerely desire a united church."

Philipp Melanchthon stroked his beard and muttered under his breath. "It is the Church of Rome we should be reuniting with."

Martin threw his black fur-lined cloak across a chair. Gold rings clacking, he grabbed a piece of chalk from his pocket and strode to the great oak table in the center of the room. It had been many years since doubt and uncertainty had caused him to ask *Are you alone wise?* Indeed, the Reformer was anything but humble about his beliefs. With great ceremony, Martin drew a large white circle in the middle of the table and scrawled *"hoc est corpus meum"* in the center and covered it with a cloth as he covered bread during the Lord's Supper. Triumphantly, he threw back his head and gestured with both hands to his dusty circle. "This is my body."[11] Martin finished with a flourish before sinking into a seat at the head of the table.

"Martin, surely you acknowledge the presence of metaphor in Scripture?" Johannes Oecolampadius of Basel sighed in frustration. "You do not mean to state that the flesh profits? For in fact, we are aware that the flesh profits nothing. Christ has ascended unto heaven. How then, tell us, can you claim the bread and wine of the Eucharist is truly the flesh and blood of Jesus?"

"You seek to prove that a body cannot be present in two places at the same time. I will not listen to proofs based on arguments derived from geometry." Martin rose to his feet and thundered to the room in general. The beating of his heart rushed through his ears and he could feel the old burn of his stomach beginning. "God is beyond all mathematics, and the words of God are to be revered and followed in awe. It is God who commands, 'Take, eat, this is my body.'" Martin brought his fist down hard upon the table, causing the chalk circle to tremor and spread slightly. "I therefore demand compelling proof from the Scriptures to the contrary."[12]

Oecolampadius widened his eyes in disbelief. "Martin, Christ compared the gospel to seed. Surely you do not think it produces literal vines!"[13]

Landgrave Philip of Hesse looked nervously about the room before catching his chancellor's eye. "Are you not to moderate here?" he whispered loudly.

The chancellor cleared his throat and stepped forward. "I believe everyone on both sides should present his arguments in a spirit of moderation."[14]

Martin glared at Oecolampadius and Zwingli before rising to his feet again. "In that case, I should like to present my case for the heresy these two learned men have been preaching in entirely other areas." Around the room there was a loud groan as scholars and theologians settled into their chairs for what promised to be a contentious meeting.

It was after three days of heated arguments that Martin sat in the small room assigned to him, gazing out the window into the crisp October evening. 1529 had been a wonderful year, with the publication of *The Large Catechism* for pastors and then *The Small Catechism* for fathers to use with their families. And there was the birth of his beloved little daughter, Magdalena. Martin had been certain that his heart would never recover from the loss of little Elizabeth before her first birthday. But small Lena touched his soul in a hidden and precious place. Her existence nearly chased the dragon from his life altogether. Yet, there was always the familiar, unbidden anger that lived just below the surface of Martin's soul.

Martin thought about the fifteen articles of faith he was to write that evening. He would summarize his teachings on creation, the Trinity, original sin, salvation, and the sacraments. Martin could not see how any agreement could be reached on the Lord's Supper. Yet, if both sides made concessions, perhaps he could soon be on the way home to see his children and his Katie. *I miss Katie. I will write her a letter.*

He picked up a pen.

Dear Katie, Our friendly conference at Marburg is almost ended, and we have agreed upon all points, except that our opponents maintain that only the bread and wine are present in the sacrament, although admitting Christ's spiritual presence in the elements. Today the Landgrave is making every effort to unite us, or at least to make us consider each other as brethren and members of Christ's body. Although we object to being brethren, we wish to live at peace and on good terms . . .

Kiss Lenchen and Hanschen for me.

Your obedient servant, Martin Luther.

P.S. They are all quite excited over the sleeping sickness. Fifty were seized yesterday, of whom two have died.[15]

Martin smiled as he considered a unified church. What a burden that would be to the Church of Rome!

A sharp rap on his cell door caused Martin to jump. Unbidden, Melanchthon entered.

"Martin, I fear you are to change your mind about the Eucharist." Melanchthon's eyes slid to the side and he shifted his weight nervously. "Our agreement about the spirit of Christ being present in the wine and the bread—rather than his actual body—it can only alienate the Holy Roman Emperor Charles V and his brother, Ferdinand. We must maintain this one point."

Martin frowned. "You, Philipp, have given me such trouble over unity and peace and now you wish to dissuade me from peace with the Protestant church? We may be one in Christ yet."

Melanchthon shook his head, his eyes roaming the small room to rest anywhere but on Martin's keen gaze. "I would have you stand strong in your convictions, Martin. You are the leader of this reformation. It will not do to stray from the Word of God."

The next morning Martin stood before the oak table in Marburg, his fifteen written articles in hand. "We have agreed to fourteen articles," he stated flatly.

Ulrich Zwingli smiled hopefully. "We have come as far as we can, Martin. We agree that Christ is present spiritually during the Eucharist. We cannot agree that the bread and wine are transformed. But we believe that your reformed claim that Christ's body and blood coexist with the bread and wine without actually changing the substance is a similar scriptural finding. We all agree there is no magic at all involved with the Eucharist. We all believe that we could sign this agreement in good faith with these teachings being close in nature."

Martin closed his eyes tightly and brushed his hand over his forehead. His brain felt addled from the rising pain in his stomach. Prior to Philipp's visit last night, his dream of a unified Protestant church had seemed so clear, so reachable. This morning, the agony of his soul etched pain through his abdomen. He had never intended to part with the pope, had he? He had only meant to follow Scripture. And now—was he sacrificing Scripture to pacify Ulrich Zwingli? What of the metaphorical nature of Scripture? Martin could hear the beating of wings as clearly as he ever had.

Martin's rings made a hollow echo on the table as he slammed his hand down on top of the articles of faith he had written. "There is to be no agreement! In this I am closer to Rome than to Switzerland!"

As the sound of his feet storming through the castle halls echoed about him, Martin swore he could hear the screech of a dragon. There was a rending in his soul as he faced the truth that once again he, Martin Luther, had witnessed a tear in the fabric of Christ's church.

Chapter 21

AND THE TRUTH GOES MARCHING ON

1530–1536

Martin paced his suite in Prince John's southernmost castle at Coburg, a few days' ride from the Imperial Diet of the Holy Roman Empire taking place in Augsburg. Little rivulets of sweat traced their way down his back. On a simple desk in the corner, his quill lay atop a fresh translation of the Psalms. Passing the desk, Martin stumbled and sank into his chair. These days, the roaring of the dragon never left his ears. It made his feet uncertain and his limbs unwilling to cooperate.

"Master Luther?" Prince John's porter stood at the door of Martin's apartment. "How is your writing going today, sir?"

Martin rubbed his head. "It is well enough, Bjorn. I have finished translating the Psalms and will begin the books of the Prophets tomorrow. I've written and published the *Sermon on Keeping Children in School*. We need even boys of lesser ability to be prepared for lives as ordinary pastors, or at the very least a ready reserve of those who would teach God's Word."[1]

The porter grinned. "I hear you are almost done with the complete translation of the Old Testament."

Martin sighed. The Old Testament was nearly translated, but he knew he would need to continue to revise the translation with the help of his friends at the University of Wittenberg. "I am now at work translating the Prophets. Good heavens! How hard it is to make the Hebrew writers speak German! They withstand our efforts, not wishing to give up their native tongue for a barbarous idiom, just as the nightingale would not change her sweet song to imitate the cuckoo whose monotonous note she abhors."[2]

Martin gazed out his window and considered the birds flying past. His thoughts turned to some of the more difficult aspects of the translation.

"I am all right on the birds of the night—owl, raven, horned owl, tawny owl, screech owl—and on the birds of prey—vulture, kite, hawk, and sparrow hawk. I can handle the stag, roebuck, and chamois, but what in the Devil am I to do with the taragelaphus, the pygargus, oryx, and camelopard?"[3]

The porter cocked his head with a confused look on his face. After a moment of awkward silence, he spotted Martin's desk and grinned. "I see you have letters for me today, Master Luther. Is that another letter for your boy? How old is he now?"

Martin smiled. "Hans is four. And his sister, Magdalena, well, here is a drawing her mother sent of her. At first I could scarcely recognize her and said, 'Dear me! Lena is so dark!' But now it pleases me well. The more I look at it, the better I see it is my Lenchen. She looks extraordinarily like Hans in the mouth, eyes, and nose, in fact in the whole face, and she will grow more like him."[4] Martin crossed the room to gaze out the window in the direction of Augsburg. "The letter tells Hans the story of a wonderful garden for children, yet he cannot enter lest he prays, studies, and is good. It must be hard on my Katie that I have been gone so often, yet she is truly lord over the Black Cloister and does not require my assistance."

The porter smiled. "Hans will enjoy the story, I'm sure. And the other letter? Where am I to deliver that, Master Luther?"

Martin frowned. The agitation at his situation returned full-force and the buzzing in his head increased. "Do you know why I'm here in this—this kingdom of the birds? Held captive here as I was at the Wartburg?"

"Sir, you are not captive! But you have no letter of safe conduct." The porter lowered his voice conspiratorially. "Sir, you are an outlaw! With Emperor Charles V in Augsburg meeting with Prince John and the other Protestant princes, this is as close as we could bring you without risking imprisonment or death."

Martin waved at the porter like he was an unwelcome fly. "Yes, well, still here I am away from my family and home for five months or more. Here." He thrust his second letter at the porter. "*To the Clergy Assembled at Augsburg.* This is my best warning to the Church of Rome. More than once I have thought we could reconcile, the pope and the Protestants. Yet now it is clear to me that is never to be. I sent Prince John to Augsburg with a list of teachings in which we differ from the teachings of the pope, all of them scriptural. Melanchthon will be writing the *Augsburg Confession*—our statement of faith. But now I feel the need to warn Charles that he must not quarrel with the Protestants. There is much dismay in Germany. The unrest is strong enough that if he outlaws the Protestant church altogether, much worse than the Peasant's War will occur. The blood will be on his own head."

"Well, the Peasant's War was horrific," the porter said, nodding. "Aye. There is much unrest. It is exactly as you say." He smiled, the gaps in his graying gums betraying the teeth that were once present. "I have a letter from home for you. Perhaps it will cheer you."

Martin handed over his letters and accepted the small package in front of him. Closing the door behind the porter, he made his way uneasily to his desk. The room dipped and spun and the roaring in his ears increased yet again. Carefully, Martin opened the letter in front of him and smoothed the paper. Glancing over the words, Martin clutched the message to his chest and fell to the floor.

"Oh, no," he cried in anguish. "Oh, my heart is moved to sorrow. That dear and gentle old man whose name I bear,[5] my father, has died." Martin began to sob. He would continue crying for two full days, long past the onset of headache and into the realm of delirium.

— — —

"There you are, rich lady of Zulsdorf, Mrs. Dr. Katharina Luther, who lives in the flesh at Wittenberg but in the spirit at Zulsdorf!"[6] Martin had purchased land, a farm, as a gift for Katie. They named the farm Zulsdorf, though Martin also called it the Sow Market in honor of the pigs Katie kept there. Martin slung his cloak back over his shoulder and bowed low in the direction of his wife. "I have been searching for you high and low. Without the children running through the halls of our Black Cloister and it being too early in the day for drinking beer with the students, the ringing in my ears becomes unbearable." Martin plodded through freshly plowed soil and lowered his considerable bulk to a large rock next to the fish pond. Three muddy toddlers were playing along the bank, digging into the mud with sticks. Overjoyed, they dropped their tools and rushed toward Martin. Aunt Lena looked on from the sandy shore.

Katie sighed and shook her pigtails. "Martin, Paul, and Margaret, do not set a finger upon your father. He has an important meeting in Eisenach he best be heading to."

Martin grimaced. "My Kette, I told you I am taken ill."

Across the field, nearly ten-year-old Hans and seven-year-old Lena looked up from their baskets of seed. "Father, you don't look terribly ill," called Lena. "You look like yourself."

Martin scowled. "Yes, well, myself is ill. I will not be meeting with Bucer or Capito. Those Strasbourg Sacramentarians can carry on in whatever manner they choose. I will not participate in their twisting of God's Word!"

Katie set her seed basket on the ground and crossed to her husband. "Martin, be reasonable. Bucer and Capito have long been your allies. The reformation must be united. Already, reform of the church is well rooted in Scotland and France. It's been twelve years since William Tyndale visited you to learn Hebrew so he could translate the English Bible."

Martin grunted. "He is still in prison."

"Yes," said Katie gently. "He will likely die for giving the common man the Word of God. Perhaps his ultimate sacrifice will occur before the end of the year." She wiped the sweat from her forehead with the back of her hand, smearing mud across her face. Looking to Hans and Lena, she gave a slight nod and they returned to their work. The toddlers had retreated to the water. Three-year-old Paul and four-year-old Martin rolled and wrestled on the bank of the pond, knocking their two-year-old sister onto her rump in the water. Margaret let out a wail and ran headlong into her mother's arms.

The girl continued to cry, large tears rolling down her chubby cheeks before splashing on Katie's shawl. Martin let out an impatient sigh. "Child, what cause have you given me to love you so? How have you deserved to be my heir? By making yourself a general nuisance. And why aren't you thankful instead of filling the garden with your howls?"[7] Little Margaret choked on her last sob and wrinkled her nose at her father.

Katie laughed. "Well, at least the good doctor can no longer hear the ringing in his ears!"

Martin heaved himself to a standing position. "What a lot of trouble there is in marriage! Adam has made a mess of our nature. Think of all the squabbles Adam and Eve must have had in the course of their nine hundred years. Eve would say, 'You ate the apple,' and Adam would retort, 'You gave it to me!'[8] I take your leave, Madame Sow Marketer. I would rather suffer abuse at the hands of Bucer than at those of my own wife."

Martin's dramatic exit was hindered by the soft plowed earth. He felt Katie's small hand on the inside of his arm. "Doctor Luther, do not be vexed. About Bucer—the reformation has begun in Denmark and Norway. It is the talk of the Wittenberg market. You know what that means for the people of those lands. There will be empty parishes and monasteries, nuns who long to escape their convents, families demanding their donated land be returned by the Church of Rome, false teaching, and persecution. There will be death, Martin. We must have strong Protestant leaders in place."

Martin's head hung low. "Kette, I do not know how long I have left to live. My head is like a knife that has had its steel honed entirely off, so that nothing is left but iron. The iron won't cut anymore—and neither will my head. I hope and pray that God will give me a good and blessed final moment."[9]

"Do not speak of your death, Doctor. But if you are to plan for the future, that must include proper unity and leadership of the church."

Martin turned, kissed his wife on the forehead and gazed at his children. His thoughts turned from the leadership of the church and the direction of the reformation back toward his health. Plagued with stomach pain, gout, and headaches, he was not certain he would live any longer than the English Bible translator William Tyndale. "I have left you everything, Kette."

He heard Katie's breath draw in sharply. "Doctor, that is not the German way."

"Regardless, you have borne my children and nursed them—you will not mismanage their property. Moreover, I think a mother is the best guardian for her children."[10] With finality, Martin strode toward home, leaving Katie staring after him.

The following morning, light played across Martin's work as he sat in his tower study in the Black Cloister. "Doctor Luther?" came a muffled voice through the heavy wooden door. "I have word from Bucer. The Strasbourg pastors assembled in Eisenach to meet with you as you requested. You did not show."

Martin bristled. His stomach rumbled in dismay. "I told them to travel to Leipzig. I will meet with them there." He fiddled with his quill, dipping it in the ink and blotting it on a sheet of paper. "I am ill."

The muffled voice was silent for a moment. "Doctor, they are here."

"What! I will not meet with them. Put them off."

"Doctor, Bucer has declared that he will not go unless you meet with him." There was a strange cough from the hallway outside.

Martin frowned, his entire face bunching like a wadded tissue. He could feel the sore on his leg weeping through the bandage. It had been four years since the terrible thing had opened and nothing any doctor could do would make it close. "Enough. Feed them and I will see them this afternoon."

There was another strangled bark from behind the door. "Doctor. I will do that."

Martin kicked the foot of his table and declared loudly to no one in particular, "The more I reconsider the matter, the less favorable I am toward this hopeless union!"

The men met later that afternoon in the living room of the Black Cloister. Martin greeted Bucer and Capito warmly, as though he had not caused them to travel more than three hundred miles from Strasbourg to be greeted by only a series of messages. He played with the large gold ring on one of his fingers, delighted to see the men taking in the details of the ornately painted panels lining the walls and ceiling of the room. Capito crossed the dining area to the great tiled stove in the corner.

"These tiles are spectacular, Martin. So detailed."

Martin moved to stand beside him. "We had this room done last year. Normally, we live as paupers, but it was a good year and we saved. This tile here, this is of Luke the Evangelist. See? He is writing his account of Christ's life in a book."

"It's extraordinary, Martin." Bucer was sincere. "Each scene is exquisite and there are many of them. What a joy it must be to share this room with your visitors."

Martin threw his shoulders back in pride. His chest—and his belly—puffed out, filling his satin tunic. "Only men are allowed here. And Katie, my wife. Someone must serve the beer." Martin laughed. "She will return from her Sow Market estate this afternoon and you will see her for dinner. Katie and the children. We have five now, you know, in addition to those we've taken in as our own. Perhaps we have eleven? Perhaps sixteen. I lose count. Sit here at the table and we will have our words."

Johannes Bucer cleared his throat and slid his slight frame behind the table. Deep lines creased his forehead and wrinkled the skin beneath his eyes. "Let us agree on the core beliefs of the Protestant church. We agree that the Scriptures are supreme and complete in authority. No man may lead the church. We look to Scripture alone."

Martin relaxed slightly. "Yes. *Sola Scriptura*—Scripture alone. On this we are agreed."

Bucer nodded. "And the only way of salvation is faith in Jesus Christ."

"Faith is a gift of God through His grace," Capito interjected.

Bucer and Martin both agreed.

Bucer continued. "Last, there is a priesthood of all believers. Every true Christian must share the gospel, read and interpret the Scriptures, and minister to believers in Christ."

Martin closed his eyes and breathed deeply. "This is all very good. We are in agreement. I had wavered in my separation with Rome, but we can agree that no one who follows the Church of Rome can agree with these three statements. We must consider the pope unsaved."

Bucer sighed, obviously relieved. "Now that we have agreed on the basic tenets of our faith, I hope we can work through our issue with the Eucharist—the Lord's Supper.

I wish to make clear that though we were present at the Marburg Colloquy in 1529, some six years ago now, Capito and I were not so strongly opposed to your final definition of the Eucharist as Zwingli and Oecolampadius were, may God rest their souls. Further, Landgrave Philip of Hesse is anxious to see a resolution to this matter so that the Protestant church may proceed in unity. We have reformed our definition of the Lord's Supper and we gave a copy to Philipp Melanchthon when we met with him just after Christmas. Did you receive our copy, Doctor?"

Martin cleared his throat. "I have. Did you see the clarification I sent with Melanchthon?" He closed his eyes and recited from memory. "Christ's body must be bitten by the teeth."[11] His eyes snapped open and the eager faces of the two men came into view. "You seek unity, but there can be no unity unless the bread and wine are said to be flesh and blood for all—believers and unbelievers alike."

Martin watched as Bucer and Capito shifted uncomfortably and glanced sideways at each other. He squinted as the light in the room seemed to grow brighter through the windowpanes. The buzz and whoosh of the dragon again sounded loudly in his ears.

"Martin . . . ," began Bucer.

Martin held up his hand. "Enough. I am faint. I will lie down, as I have repeatedly told you I am not well. Katie will serve you tonight and you may instruct my students in anything but the Lord's Supper. We will meet in the morning." Martin stumbled to his feet and raced to his bedroom to spend a sleepless night imagining the destruction of Christ's newly reformed church.

In the morning, he dressed cautiously, the hum of wings a constant companion in his ears. After praying earnestly for a time, just as he did every morning, the former monk joined his guests in the dining hall of the great monastery. "We must begin again. We must agree that all are without worth and none is deserving of taking the Lord's Supper."

Bucer and Capito nodded joyously.

Hours later, the three men sat back in their chairs at the dining table. They had exchanged many words; the meaning of each was distant and clouded, like a horizon just before a thunderstorm arrives. Yet Martin could not shake the feeling of urgency he had been plagued with all night. *We are not opposed, even if we are not agreed.*

Lumbering around the table, Martin pulled Bucer from his chair and embraced him. Doing the same to Capito, he laughed heartily. "There, see? We will part brothers in Christ after all. Kaaatiiee! My brothers and I are in need of beer. Not so much beer as my dear friend, the new prince of Saxony, the young John Frederick." He slapped Bucer on the shoulder. "We have been blessed with a prince who has many fine gifts. But if I were to drink as much as the elector, I'd drown. If he drank as much as I, he'd die of thirst."[12] Martin chuckled heartily and gathered steins for his guests while Bucer and Capito burst into tears of joy.

Agreement on doctrine was elusive, but for now the Protestants had united.

Chapter 22

TABLE TALKS IN THE BLACK CLOISTER

1537–1542

A haa! It hurts dreadfully! Do not make me drink another stein of water, beer, or wine. I shall drown like the animals left outside the ark. I shall burst. Call Johannes Bugenhagen that I may make a will. John Frederick, you will find the articles I've written on the desk in the corner. Aaahh!"

The princes' physicians gathered in a corner of Martin's room and whispered amongst themselves. Martin groaned in agony as two of them departed. A small crowd of German theologians and princes gathered just inside the door in the little room in Schmalkalden in February 1537. Martin felt certain no one wished to miss being present for the death of the infamous reformer. *If nothing else, it shall be a historic moment. I should like to witness it myself were I they.*

"Our dear Lord God will have mercy on us for his name's sake and he will extend your life, dear Doctor."[1] Prince John Frederick shifted his weight and wrinkled his brow. "These kidney stones will move. And we will take your articles, your outline of the teachings of the Protestant church, before the Schmalkaldic League for approval."

The two doctors returned with a bowl of foul-smelling material. One approached Martin to administer the new medication. Martin's stomach, already roiling in distress, turned violently, making him feel as though he may lose every bit of liquid he had been forced to swallow.

"What is that stench? Do not tell me this is the way you treat the princes and their families!"

The doctor stepped forward, in spite of Martin's anger. "This is designed to cause discomfort and force the stone out of your body, Doctor. You must eat it all."

Martin squeezed his eyes tight and chewed while Johannes Bugenhagen arrived and prayed for him. The tired pastor gagged, then joined the prayer with one of his own for the princes, scholars, and ministers who would carry on the fight to share the gospel and look to Scripture after his death. He turned to Bugenhagen. "Command them in my name that they should act with confidence in God for the course of the gospel in whatever way the Holy Spirit might suggest."[2]

Bugenhagen nodded solemnly. "I will, Martin."

Martin turned to the physician who had prepared another batch of the horrible-tasting herbal remedy. "What is that, man? I must know what you are feeding a dying man!"

The doctor stepped back several steps. "Garlic, Doctor."

"I've never had garlic that looked like that. What else is in your bowl?"

"Horse manure, Doctor. It will force the stone out."

Martin roared in the direction of the physicians. The act wore him out and he collapsed on the bed. "Take me home. Send me back to Saxony and my Wittenberg. I will see my family before I die!"

The road home was a trail of agony for Martin. He lay in a cart and bounced over every rut and pothole for nearly ten miles before reaching an inn. Stumbling toward a straw mat on the floor, he reversed course and made it to an outhouse nearby. Many minutes later, Martin emerged, weak and in pain, but no longer on death's door.

By summer, Martin's recovery was progressing nicely. His children ran about on the lawn of the Black Cloister in the bright sunlight, along with eight of his nieces and nephews who also lived in the large monastery. Martin had given them time off from their studies, and all six tutors had been sent to spend the afternoon in the town square. The garden was occupied by small groups of students and visitors. Several of the guests had taken up residence in the Black Cloister for various lengths of time. Katie sat beneath Martin's favorite pear tree, poring over the financial books for her Zulsdorf property, the "Sow Market," her gift from Martin.

"My beloved wife, Katharina, Mrs. Dr. Luther, mistress of the pig market, lady of Zulsdorf," Martin looked askance, "and whatever other titles may befit thy Grace."[3] He bowed low before his wife and dropped a small bag of money in her lap. "I have come into some money. Of course, I have given some of it away. But the rest I bring to you, O keeper of our household, cloister, farm, and other various properties."

Katie rolled her eyes. "Martin, you are hopeless. It is a wonder we eat with the money you give away. Not only that, but I cannot convince you to accept money for the books you write, a salary for your teaching, nor will you agree to charge these motley students of yours for the wisdom they copy from you at the dinner table every night."

"Ah, dear Kette. We are poor, yet the Lord sustains us." Martin turned from the conversation, unwilling to discuss the matter further with his wife. "Who will bowl with me?" The priest strode across the lawn and retrieved a stone ball. Several of the meandering students as well as Hans and Lena cheered and moved toward Martin. "Someone set up the pins for me. Just nine, as I've said before. Let us imagine they are our sins to be slain!"

Eight-year-old Lena giggled and moved closer to her father. "Oh, Papa, you are so very funny." Martin looked at the young girl and smiled. Lena was the joy of his life. A sparkling little girl, she was the picture of health and life. His love for her was as wide and open as the unclouded sky.

The group bowled together throughout the afternoon, joking loudly enough to draw attention from College Street. As they gathered in the Black Cloister for dinner, Martin became aware of a visitor in the entryway.

"Capito! You've come a long way. You must have dinner with us and stay as long as you wish."

Capito smiled and followed Martin into the dining area.

At dinner that evening, Martin filled the room with advice on every subject he could think of. Students asked questions and concentrated on his answers, filing the information in their brains to fill pages of journals with writing later that night in their rooms. Martin enjoyed the attention immensely. Throughout the dining hall, children laughed and side conversations added to the din. Every dinner at the Black Cloister was a gathering of thirty people or more.

After the meal, Capito pulled Martin aside in the stone hallway outside the living room. Stacks of Martin's paperwork and books overflowed from wooden tables and correspondence spilled off a row of chairs along the wall. "Martin, before we part, I wish to address one last issue with you. As you are aware, I am known for my work in the Hebrew language."

Martin laughed. "Brother, you are one of the best Hebrew scholars in all of Europe. I would love to have you on our team of scholars to complete the translation of the Old Testament. I am certain that if I ask, the good Prince John Frederick would approve your transfer to the University of Wittenberg. The boy is quite fond of my teachings."

Capito shifted awkwardly. "Thank you, Doctor. However, my concern is with the Jewish people. As you know, the Jews have long been banned from Spain and dreadfully abused there. Just eight months ago, in August of 1536, Prince John Frederick expelled the Jews from Saxony and has prevented them from even traveling through our country on their way to search for freedom. I've come on behalf of the scholar Joel Rosheim—he is a Jew—to ask for your assistance. We know you wrote *That Jesus Christ Was Born a Jew* in support of the Jewish people more than a decade ago. It is true that Jesus, too, was a Jew. Will you go to the elector for us?"

Martin adjusted his ring as he thought. It was true that he had been a defender of the Jewish people. He had reached out to them with the true gospel. And yet, they had denied the chance to follow the true Messiah. The old ugly heat from his belly lit a fire in his veins. He glared at Capito and the man took a step backward.

"The Jewish people have so shamefully abused everything I have done.[4] I will write a letter to Rosheim myself. In fact, I will write a letter against the Jews and publish it. They have denied the gospel of Christ."

Capito gasped. "But doctor, could they not yet be converted? Are they not made in the image of God? As any unbeliever, are the Jews not precious and valuable? Doctor, I have come hundreds of miles to ask for your help."

"Then you have come in vain. For I will write a letter and publish it."

Capito's usually placid face colored. His brows creased and spittle flew from his mouth. "Doctor Luther, you are wrong here. In this, you do not defend Scripture. You do not defend Christ. Rather, you harm a people who need our love. We have been commanded to love even our enemies. Does that not include the Jews? At the end of your life, this foul act will mar your place in history. I beg you to reconsider."

Martin bristled. He had fought long and hard for Scripture, and those who could not see his view of Scripture must be wrong. The ringing in his head reached new and epic proportions and his vision blurred slightly. "I will write the letter. What's more, I will write about the Anabaptists, too, just as I have written about those who follow the Church of Rome. They do not subscribe to the one, true gospel."

Capito turned his head and spit on the ground. "Your words, Doctor Luther, have been used by God to reform the church. Take care they are not used also by Satan to cause the deaths of many."

Martin turned to see Katie standing in the hallway, silently observing. Capito pushed past him toward Katie and bowed. "Frau Luther, I will not be staying here this evening. I wish you well." With that, the scholar left. His words joined the bells ringing in Martin's head.

———

Five years passed as Martin wrote letters, booklets, and sermons. He preached on Galatians, became involved in controversies in the church and politics, and worked with other Protestant leaders to hammer out the details of the new church's beliefs. When the Roman church began to talk of reform, Martin pushed to be present at their meetings. When they declined, his suspicion increased. Martin's children matured, and Hans, now sixteen years old, was sent to Torgau with his teacher to learn how to be a doctor.

———

Martin examined the face of his wife. At forty-three, she was beginning to age slightly and the smile lines around her mouth had deepened. Today, they were turned downward like grass blowing in the wind before a storm.

"Hans should come home from school immediately." Martin picked up his quill. "Lena is seriously ill."

"Yes. Right away," Katie said. "I shall get someone to care for the animals for me."

Martin nodded. The Sow Market was not important at a time like this. However, the animals could not fend for themselves.

"How many do we have now?" he asked Katie. Martin wrote his letter to Hans in short, staccato bursts of ink.

"Animals? Five cows, nine calves, three goats." Katie's voice cracked. "And the pigs. There are ten of them."

Martin dropped his quill on the table, splattering ink along the wall. Embracing his wife, he rested his damp cheek on her head covering. "Dear Katie. Remember where she came from. She is faring well."[5]

Katie buried her face in Martin's tunic and began to sob. "She came from the Lord, Doctor, but I do not wish to return her."

Martin held his wife while she sobbed and thought of his beloved Magdalena, her thirteen-year-old body lying in a bed, wracked with fever. A storm broke loose from his eyes and the thunder in his stomach clouded his heart.

TWILIGHT AND A CAKE

September 1542–February 18, 1546

Magdalena, my dear little daughter, would you like to stay here with your father?" Martin turned his attention to the fall scene outside Magdalena's room and prayed for strength. "Or would you willingly go to your Father yonder?"[1] He set his gentle gaze upon the face of his beloved Lena, who held a spot in his heart unavailable to any other. Her face was sallow and sunken after months of illness.

"Darling father, as God wills."[2] Lena's voice was distant and fading.

From across the room, Martin heard a sob die in Katie's chest before it found life in the brisk morning air.

Taking his precious girl in his arms, Martin bowed his head. "I love her very much. I am angry with myself that I cannot rejoice in heart and be thankful as I ought."[3] Rocking his daughter, Martin prayed and stroked her hair until Magdalena ceased drawing breath.

In a strangled scream, Katie collapsed to the floor. The physician was instantly by her side. Unable to suppress the roiling clouds of despair any longer, Martin succumbed. Gently lowering Lena's body to the bed, he fled for his room in the tower, leaving his wife to sob for days in her own storm of misery.

— ■ —

"Away with this Sodom!"[4] Martin stood to face the prince. He could feel the old burn of passion deep within his chest, but it no longer gave him strength. Instead, it seemed to drain the energy from his body. "John Frederick, Wittenberg makes a mockery of God with those terrible Roman dresses and dances that no Christian has the right to attend. The Renaissance is a plague upon our fair Germany. I have already written my dear Katie instructing her to sell all we own and join me."

"And to where will you go, Martin? Where do you intend to travel where sin will not reach your tender self?" John Frederick sighed. Martin could see the annoyance etched in his features. "Honestly, Doctor, this is much like the time you announced to your congregation that their ongoing sins annoyed you. You left the pulpit and refused to speak for eight weeks. Do you remember?"

Martin stuck out his lower jaw and glared at the thick trestle table in the home of his friend like a petulant child. "Yes."

John Frederick's eyes narrowed and Martin imagined him as a great beast moving in for the kill. Outside, a thunderclap was followed by the sound of a steady downpour. "Martin, are you yourself without sin? Just five years ago you advised Landgrave Philip of Hesse to take a secret second wife rather than divorcing his own Christine. What an infernal dung heap, Doctor. Your advice was questionable at best, and the validity of our movement was seriously threatened."

Martin sunk lower in his chair, chastened by the Prince of Saxony.

John Frederick continued his speech, his tone a touch gentler. "Doctor, you are angry and rash. You hold to Scripture alone, yet require that every understanding of the true meaning of Scripture stand with your interpretation. Should anyone cross you, your anger is unparalleled. You are like an enraged firedrake descending upon a town. You are a lightning bolt, Martin."

Martin sighed with drama and felt that even the air he exhaled had grown heavy. "Elector, I have become old. I am sixty-one, and I am tired. My heart hurts and has grown weak. Set me free from service to the people of that stinking sandpit. It has been long enough."

The prince stood to his feet. "I will not, Doctor Luther. You have set in motion the reform of the church. You must return to Wittenberg and continue in your duty. It is your calling to finish the work before you. I will wait outside and we shall return together."

Martin laid his head in his hands, elbows on his knees. It had been a nice dream, if only a momentary one. The idea of living the rest of his days in isolation with his family, free of exposure to the sins of others and the pain of leadership was tempting. Yet, John Frederick was right. Martin had a duty to do. He sighed heavily again and lumbered onto his feet.

The journey home was a quiet one, and Martin had much time to think about the events of the last years. There had been his angry letters published against the Roman church and the pope, against the Anabaptists and the Jews, letters about war and princes, kings and emperors. There was that business with Landgrave Philip of Hesse as well. Martin had been so confused. He was certain divorce was unscriptural. Yet, men in the Scriptures had taken more than one wife. Even so, those situations had not seemed blessed by God. In fact, the results had often been disastrous. Martin squeezed his eyes tightly in regret while a wave of nausea washed over him. Katie had been so enraged when he gave into Philip's pressure and issued the secret permission to marry a second wife. She had promised that should Martin ever take another bride, she would leave him with the children and property to manage alone. A tear rolled down Martin's cheek. He turned in the carriage to watch the German countryside roll past.

As the carriage approached the Black Cloister, Martin saw his family gathered in the summer sun, bowling and laughing. He swung his gout-ridden legs to the ground and limped toward them without a wave to the elector. Martin,

Paul, and Margaret surrounded their father and cheered his arrival.

Later that night, Martin buried his head in Katie's shoulder. "Aw, Kette." Regret flowed over Martin like a hot summer wind. "Wrath just will not let go of me. Why, I sometimes rage about a silly little thing not worth mentioning. Whoever crosses my path has to pay for it, and I won't say a kind word to anyone. Isn't that shameful? I might be entitled to other sins, material comforts for example, but I let some trifle get me all worked up!"[5] The great German doctor sobbed in despair.

"Doctor, you must not despair. The Lord has raised you up for such a time as this."

Martin pulled away, drying his tears on the palms of his fleshy hands. "Madame Sow Marketer, it is enough. I am an exhausted old man, tired out from so many labors. I have worked myself to death. For one person, I have done enough. I'll go lie down in the sand and sleep now. It is over for me, except for just an occasional little whack at the pope."[6]

Katie wrinkled her nose. "Dearest Doctor, I should think you would find someplace better to lie than in the stinking sand dune along the Elbe River. For it's muddy and the slaughterhouse upwind causes it to reek." She giggled.

Martin laughed. "You, woman, think yourself wise merely because you manage the pigs!"

The remaining summer and autumn of 1545 passed without event. Martin did the duty he was called to, preaching and writing. In November, nineteen-year-old Hans returned home in time for a grand birthday party

Katie threw for Martin on the tenth day of the month. Fourteen-year-old Martin, twelve-year-old Paul, and ten-year-old Margaret attended, filling Martin's sixty-two-year-old heart with pride. The old monk smiled to think of the blessings of family and home he had nearly missed in his desperate effort to be saved according to his works as a monk.

The party was a grand and joyous event. The next morning Martin climbed into the pulpit of his beloved town church. His voice sounded deep and tired even to his own ears. "This is my dear Genesis. God grant that others do better with it after me—I can do no more—I am weak. Pray God will grant to me a good, blessed final hour."[7] Martin looked over the faces of his audience and smiled. Dear friends and colleagues, students and townspeople smiled back at him, tears in their eyes.

A few months later, in January 1546, Martin took his friend Justus Jonas with him to mediate a dispute between the three counts of Mansfeld, all brothers and all angry. Katie begged Martin not to leave, sobbing and arguing that he was far too old and Eisleben was too far to travel in the bitter German winter. Martin left anyway. His need to be involved was far too great to be halted by inconsequential details such as ice chunks tossing about in the swollen Salle River. Martin hadn't told Katie, but he'd written each count multiple times asking to mediate their dispute until finally they had all given in, inviting him to come.

Martin sat by the window and chuckled over the letter he had written to Katie. Her letters had been full of anxiety for Martin's safety. To mock her, he described a series of horrendous events occurring.

Most holy lady doctoress! I thank you kindly for your great anxiety which keeps you awake. Since you began to worry we have almost had a fire at the inn, just in front of my door, and yesterday, due to your anxiety no doubt, a stone nearly fell on my head which would have squeezed it up as a trap does a mouse. For this I thank your anxiety, but the dear angels protected me. I fear that unless you stop worrying the earth will swallow me up or the elements will persecute me.[8]

Martin smiled as he folded the letter, his sixth to Katie since arriving in Eisleben, and carefully addressed it with a string of titles he reserved only for his wife. Looking out the window at the mid-February snow, Martin closed his eyes as the old weariness washed over him. The counts had agreed upon a solution to their dispute only just this morning. Afterward, Martin had strengthened them in Scripture before rushing to his room to recover from a sudden bout of weakness. Returning to his bed, Martin collapsed and willed the room to stop spinning. He frowned as his heart began to thump quickly in his chest, like the heart of a man who had run from Wittenberg to Eisleben. Martin prayed for a moment before calling out in alarm.

"I need help! A physician—I need a physician!" Martin heard thumping down the hallway outside his room. He murmured, "Oh, that my Katie was here. She is twice the physician of any doctor in Germany."

Count Albrecht had his personal doctor supply Martin with medicine to calm his furious heart. Martin sighed as his body relaxed and slipped into a deep sleep. From beside him he heard Jonas promise to remain with a large group of men in the next room over where they could hear calls for help in case Martin needed anything.

The moon was shining brightly when Martin next opened his eyes. Sitting suddenly in the bed, he clutched his chest while eerie shadows chased each other across the wall. "Oh, dear Lord God!" Martin prayed in screams. "My pain is so great!" He clawed at his ribcage and gasped for breath. In the next room there was a wild scuffling noise and the door to his room burst open. "Oh, dear Jonas, I think I shall remain here at Eisleben where I was born and baptized!"[9]

Jonas rushed to Martin's side, supporting him from behind. Martin struggled to focus on the faces of those filling the room. Giving up, he focused instead on the Christ he loved. "For God so loved the world," Martin's breath came in ragged staccato bursts. "That he gave his only begotten Son[10] that whosoever believeth in him should not perish, but have everlasting life." Martin coughed roughly and pulled air through his parted lips before beginning again. "For God so loved the world . . ."

On his third time through the verse, Martin became aware of breath in his ear. "Martin," came the voice of Justus Jonas. Martin's vision was dark with floating white sparks crossing like jagged flashes of lightning between storm clouds. "Martin, will you stand steadfast by Christ and the doctrine you have preached?"[11]

Martin gasped in agony. "Ja!"[12]

The storm clouds and lightning cleared from Martin's vision as the heart of the monk who did battle with dragons burst. The hand that hammered the *Ninety-Five Theses* to the door of an old German church fluttered before lying still. Martin Luther, father of the Reformation, lay in the sand to sleep.

AUTHOR'S NOTE

Martin Luther once said: "I simply taught, preached, and wrote God's Word. And while I slept or drank Wittenberg beer with my friends Philip and Amsdorf, the Word so greatly weakened the papacy that no prince or emperor ever inflicted such losses on it. I did nothing. The Word did everything."[1]

Martin Luther was a complicated character. He was gentle and kind, and yet he could be crude and angry. God used Luther in a mighty way to call people to Himself through Scripture. Luther is often called the "Father of the Reformation" because of the part he played in promoting Scripture alone, faith alone, and grace alone through Christ alone to the glory of God alone. Would Luther have been effective had he been a gentler, kinder soul in our contemporary estimation? No one can say. Martin Luther certainly didn't think so. He believed God chose him *because* of his fiery spirit. We can trust that God is sovereign over history.

Writing a narrative work on Martin Luther was not easy. In telling his story, I left a lot of details out. Also, I changed or invented details to keep the story flowing. Many of the quotes Luther speaks in this book were actually written in letters to friends and colleagues. For the sake of clarity and narrative, I omitted both people and historical details from Luther's life. Some characters aren't named with certainty. For example, we know that as a college student, Luther had a friend named Hieronymus Buntz who died during the plague. We also know that Luther lost two friends to typhoid fever. Was Buntz with Luther when he slipped and stabbed himself? That we do not know. We know only that he was traveling with a friend.

My goal in telling Luther's story was to be faithful to history, to Scripture, and yet to remain brutally honest. If you are interested in further study on Martin Luther, you will find there are a great many books about him. I've heard it said that he is the second-most-written-about person in history. Jesus Christ has, of course, been written about more often than any human ever to live. You may want to start your research with two biographies on Luther that I found to be readable and engaging. Roland H. Bainton's 1950 classic, *Here I Stand: A Life of Martin Luther* (reprinted by Hendrickson, 2009), is interesting and well written. Likewise, *Luther the Reformer: The Story of the Man and His Career* by James M. Kittelson (Augsburg, 1986) is a good read.

Martin Luther dedicated his life to the fight for the true gospel. His struggle to lead the church back to the authority of Scripture must not go unheeded. Let's not forget his efforts, and let us not grow complacent about the wonderful gift of God's Word in our own lives and fellowships.

Soli Deo Gloria,
Danika Cooley

NOTES

Chapter 2

1. Roland H. Bainton, *Here I Stand: A Life of Martin Luther*, Hendrickson Classic Biographies (Peabody, MA: Hendrickson, 2009 [1950]), 8.
2. Missal of Paul III (1534–1549). From: N. A. "Confiteor," https://en.wikipedia.org/wiki/Confiteor.

Chapter 3

1. Preserved Smith, PhD, *The Life and Letters of Martin Luther* (Boston and New York: Houghton Mifflin, 1911), 4.
2. Ibid.
3. 1 Sam. 1:1-2 (KJV).
4. Rev. Heemann Fick, *The Life and Deeds of Martin Luther*, trans. Rev. Prof. M. Loy (Columbus, OH: J. A. Schulze, 1869), 18.

Chapter 6

1. Rev. Heemann Fick, *The Life and Deeds of Martin Luther*, trans. Rev. Prof. M. Loy (Columbus, OH: J. A. Schulze, 1869), 21–22.

Chapter 6

1. Roland H. Bainton, *Here I Stand: A Life of Martin Luther*, Hendrickson Classic Biographies (Peabody, MA: Hendrickson, 2009 [1950]), 15.

2. Arthur Cushman McGiffert, *Martin Luther: The Man and His Work* (New York: The Century Co., 1911), 24.

3. Rev. Heemann Fick, *The Life and Deeds of Martin Luther*, trans. Rev. Prof. M. Loy (Columbus, OH: J. A. Schulze, 1869), 38.

4. Bainton, *Here I Stand*, 21.

Chapter 7

1. Preserved Smith, PhD, *The Life and Letters of Martin Luther* (Boston and New York: Houghton Mifflin, 1911), sec. 10 (excerpt of Luther's letter to John Braun, April 22, 1507).

2. Ibid.

3. Rev. Heemann Fick, *The Life and Deeds of Martin Luther*, trans. Rev. Prof. M. Loy (Columbus, OH: J. A. Schulze, 1869), 38.

4. Smith, *Life and Letters*, 11.

5. Fick, *Life and Deeds*, 49.

6. Roland H. Bainton, *Here I Stand: A Life of Martin Luther*, Hendrickson Classic Biographies (Peabody, MA: Hendrickson, 2009 [1950]), 33.

Chapter 8

1. Preserved Smith, PhD, *The Life and Letters of Martin Luther* (Boston and New York: Houghton Mifflin, 1911), sec. 18.

2. Rev. Heemann Fick, *The Life and Deeds of Martin Luther*, trans. Rev. Prof. M. Loy (Columbus, OH: J. A. Schulze, 1869), 57.

3. Ibid., 58.

4. Roland H. Bainton, *Here I Stand: A Life of Martin Luther*, Hendrickson Classic Biographies (Peabody, MA: Hendrickson, 2009 [1950]), 32.

Chapter 9

1. Preserved Smith, PhD, *The Life and Letters of Martin Luther* (Boston and New York: Houghton Mifflin, 1911), sec. 14.

2. Roland H. Bainton, *Here I Stand: A Life of Martin Luther*, Hendrickson Classic Biographies (Peabody, MA: Hendrickson, 2009 [1950]), 39.

3. Ibid., 40–41.

4. Ibid., 41.

5. Ibid.

6. Charlotte Mary Yonge, *Cameos from English History: The Wars of the Roses*, 3rd series (London: Macmillan & Co., 1877), 348.

7. Rev. Heemann Fick, *The Life and Deeds of Martin Luther*, trans. Rev. Prof. M. Loy (Columbus, OH: J. A. Schulze, 1869), 64.

8. Martin Luther, *The Letters of Martin Luther*, trans. Margaret A. Currie (London: Macmillan & Co., 1908), Letter IX, to John Lange, October 26, 1516.

9. Fick, *Life and Deeds*, 52.

Chapter 10

1. Edwin P. Booth, *Martin Luther: The Great Reformer* (Uhrichsville, OH: Barbour and Co., 1995), 76.

2. James M. Kittelson, *Luther the Reformer: The Story of the Man and His Career* (Minneapolis: Augsburg, 1986), 93.

3. Roland H. Bainton, *Here I Stand: A Life of Martin Luther*, Hendrickson Classic Biographies (Peabody, MA: Hendrickson, 2009 [1950]), 48.

4. Ibid.

5. Martin Luther, *The Letters of Martin Luther*, trans. Margaret A. Currie (London: Macmillan & Co., 1908), Letter IX, to John Lange, October 26, 1516.

6. Ibid., Letter XVI, to Albert of Mainz, October 31, 1517.

Chapter 11

1. Martin Luther, *The Letters of Martin Luther*, trans. Margaret A. Currie (London: Macmillan & Co., 1908), Letter XVI, to Albert of Mainz, October 31, 1517.

2. Preserved Smith, PhD, *The Life and Letters of Martin Luther* (Boston and New York: Houghton Mifflin, 1911), 41–42 (thesis 50).

3. Ibid., 24.

4. Martin Luther, *Works of Martin Luther*, "Disputation of Doctor Martin Luther on the Power and Efficacy of Indulgences— 1517*, vol. 1, trans. Adolph Spaeth, L. D. Reed, Henry Eyster Jacobs, et al. (Philadelphia: A. J. Holman Co., 1915), 29–38 (theses 20, 26).

5. Ibid., thesis 82.

6. Ibid., theses 75, 76.

7. Ibid., theses 62, 63, 64.

8. Ibid., theses 65, 66.

9. Ibid., theses 1, 6, 36, 45, 54, 86, 94, 95.

10. Luther, *Letters of Martin Luther*, Letter XVI, to Albert of Mainz, October 31, 1517.

11. Ibid.

12. Ibid.

13. Ibid.

Chapter 12

1. James M. Kittelson, *Luther the Reformer: The Story of the Man and His Career* (Minneapolis: Augsburg, 1986), 115.

2. Martin Luther, *Luther's Correspondence and Other Contemporary Letters*, vol. 1, trans. and ed. Preserved Smith, PhD (Philadephia: The Lutheran Publication Society, 1913), Letter 60, Luther to Spalatin, May 18, 1518.

3. Kittelson, *Luther the Reformer*, 114.

4. Ibid., 117 (one sentence only).

5. E. G. Schwiebert, *Luther and His Times: The Reformation from a New Perspective* (St. Louis: Concordia, 1950), 347.

6. Rev. Heemann Fick, *The Life and Deeds of Martin Luther*, trans. Rev. Prof. M. Loy (Columbus, OH: J. A. Schulze, 1869), 88.

7. Preserved Smith, PhD, *The Life and Letters of Martin Luther* (Boston and New York: Houghton Mifflin, 1911), 50.

8. Ibid., 50–51.

9. Roland H. Bainton, *Here I Stand: A Life of Martin Luther*, Hendrickson Classic Biographies (Peabody, MA: Hendrickson, 2009 [1950]), 79.

10. Ibid.

11. Ibid., 79–80.

12. Ibid., 80.

13. Fick, *Life and Deeds*, 90.

14. Luther, *Luther's Correspondence*, Letter 85, Luther to Karlstadt, October 14, 1518, 119.

15. Ibid.

Chapter 13

1. Martin Luther, *Luther's Correspondence and Other Contemporary Letters*, vol. 1, trans. and ed. Preserved Smith, PhD (Philadephia: The Lutheran Publication Society, 1913), Letter 103, Luther to Spalatin, December 9, 1518, 137.

2. Ibid., Letter 120, Luther to Frederick, c. January 19, 1519.

3. James M. Kittelson, *Luther the Reformer: The Story of the Man and His Career* (Minneapolis: Augsburg, 1986), 139.

4. Preserved Smith, PhD, *The Life and Letters of Martin Luther* (Boston and New York: Houghton Mifflin, 1911), letter, Luther to Spalatin, July 20, 1519, 65.

5. Roland H. Bainton, *Here I Stand: A Life of Martin Luther* (Peabody, MA: Hendrickson, 2009 [1950]), 100.

6. Ibid.

7. Ibid., 102.

8. Smith, *Life and Letters*, 63.

9. Bainton, *Here I Stand*, 105.

10. Ibid.

11. E. G. Schwiebert, *Luther and His Times: The Reformation from a New Perspective* (St. Louis: Concordia, 1950), 412 (paraphrased).

12. Ibid.

Chapter 14

1. Preserved Smith, PhD, *The Life and Letters of Martin Luther* (Boston and New York: Houghton Mifflin, 1911), letter, Luther to Spalatin, July 10, 1520, 75.

2. Ruth A. Tucker, *Parade of Faith: A Biographical History of the Christian Church* (Grand Rapids: Zondervan, 2011), 226.

3. Smith, *Life and Letters*, letter, Von Hutten to Luther, June 4, 1520, 74.

4. Ibid., letter, Luther to Spalatin, July 10, 1520, 74–75 (last two sentences).

5. James M. Kittelson, *Luther the Reformer: The Story of the Man and His Career* (Minneapolis: Augsburg, 1986), 149 (last sentence only).

6. Smith, *Life and Letters*, 97.

7. Roland H. Bainton, *Here I Stand: A Life of Martin Luther*, Hendrickson Classic Biographies (Peabody, MA: Hendrickson, 2009 [1950]), 138.

8. Ibid., 155.

9. Martin Luther, *The Harvard Classics*, vol. 36, *Concerning Christian Liberty (1520)*, trans. R. S. Grignon (New York: P. F. Collier & Son, 1910), 353–97.

10. Church of England, "Te Deum," *Book of Common Prayer* (London: Eyre & Spottiswoode, 1892).

11. Smith, *Life and Letters*, 100.

12. Bainton, *Here I Stand*, 158.

Chapter 15

1. Preserved Smith, PhD, *The Life and Letters of Martin Luther* (Boston and New York: Houghton Mifflin, 1911), letter, Luther to Spalatin, December 21, 1520, 105.

2. Edwin P. Booth, *Martin Luther: The Great Reformer* (Uhrichsville, OH: Barbour and Co., 1995), 110.

3. Smith, *Life and Letters*, letter, Luther to Spalatin, December 21, 1520, 105.

4. Ibid.

5. Ibid., letter, Luther to Spalatin, April 14, 1521, 111.

6. Ibid., 104.

7. Martin Luther, *Luther's Correspondence and Other Contemporary Letters*, vol. 1, trans. and ed. Preserved Smith, PhD (Philadephia: The Lutheran Publication Society, 1913), Letter 448, Aleander to the Vice-Chancellor Cardinal d'Medici, April 16, 1521, 522.

8. Ibid., Letter 452, Aleander to the Vice-Chancellor Cardinal d'Medici, April 17, 1521, 526.

9. Ibid.

10. Smith, *Life and Letters*, 113.

11. Ibid.

12. Ibid., Letter, Luther to Cuspinian, April 17, 1521, 114.

13. Ibid., 115.

14. Ibid.

15. Ibid., 116.

16. Roland H. Bainton, *Here I Stand: A Life of Martin Luther*, Hendrickson Classic Biographies (Peabody, MA: Hendrickson, 2009 [1950]), 179.

17. Smith, *Life and Letters*, 116.

18. Ibid., 117.

19. Ibid., 118.

20. E. G. Schwiebert, *Luther and His Times: The Reformation from a New Perspective* (St. Louis: Concordia, 1950), 505.

21. Smith, *Life and Letters*, 118.

22. Schwiebert, *Luther and His Times*, 506.

23. Luther, *Luther's Correspondence*, Letter 465, Luther to Emperor Charles V, April 28, 1521, 548.

Chapter 16

1. Martin Luther, *The Letters of Martin Luther*, trans. Margaret A. Currie (London: Macmillan & Co., 1908), Letter LIX, Luther to Melanchthon, May 12, 1521, 73.

2. Rev. Heemann Fick, *The Life and Deeds of Martin Luther*, trans. Rev. Prof. M. Loy (Columbus, OH: J. A. Schulze, 1869), 113.

3. Preserved Smith, PhD, *The Life and Letters of Martin Luther* (Boston and New York: Houghton Mifflin, 1911), letter, Luther to Spalatin, December 21, 1521, 130.

4. James M. Kittelson, *Luther the Reformer: The Story of the Man and His Career* (Minneapolis: Augsburg, 1986), 175.

5. Ibid., 286.

Chapter 17

1. James M. Kittelson, *Luther the Reformer: The Story of the Man and His Career* (Minneapolis: Augsburg, 1986), 182.

2. Ibid.

3. Ibid., 186.

4. Roland H. Bainton, *Here I Stand: A Life of Martin Luther*, Hendrickson Classic Biographies (Peabody, MA: Hendrickson, 2009 [1950]), 292.

Chapter 18

1. Preserved Smith, PhD, *The Life and Letters of Martin Luther* (Boston and New York: Houghton Mifflin, 1911), 172.

2. Roland H. Bainton, *Here I Stand: A Life of Martin Luther*, Hendrickson Classic Biographies (Peabody, MA: Hendrickson, 2009 [1950]), 265.

3. Mark Galli, "From the Editor: The Forgotten Years of Martin Luther," *Christian History* 39 (1993), https://www.christianhistoryinstitute.org/magazine/article/forgotten-years-of-martin-luther/.

4. James Harvey Robinson, *Readings in European History*, vol. 2 (Boston: Ginn & Co., 1906), 106–8.

5. Ibid.

6. Smith, *Life and Letters*, 174–75.

Chapter 19

1. Steven Ozment, "A Monk Marries: Luther's Wit and Wisdom about His New Estate," *Christian History* 39 (1993): 24.

2. Steven Ozment, "Reinventing Family Life," *Christian History* 39 (1993), https://www.christianhistoryinstitute.org /magazine/article/reinventing-family-life/.

3. Roland H. Bainton, *Here I Stand: A Life of Martin Luther*, Hendrickson Classic Biographies (Peabody, MA: Hendrickson, 2009 [1950]), 297.

4. James M. Kittelson, *Luther the Reformer: The Story of the Man and His Career* (Minneapolis: Augsburg, 1986), 205.

5. Preserved Smith, PhD, *The Life and Letters of Martin Luther* (Boston and New York: Houghton Mifflin, 1911), 208.

6. Ozment, "Reinventing Family Life."

7. Bainton, *Here I Stand*, 80.

8. Martin Luther, "A Mighty Fortress Is Our God," trans. Frederick H. Hedge, hymn 67 in *The Methodist Hymnal* (Nashville: The Methodist Book Concern, 1939).

Chapter 20

1. Roland H. Bainton, *Here I Stand: A Life of Martin Luther*, Hendrickson Classic Biographies (Peabody, MA: Hendrickson, 2009 [1950]).

2. Ibid.

3. Martin Luther, *A Short Exposition of Dr. Martin Luther's Small Catechism* (St. Louis: Concordia, 1912), 3.

4. Ibid.

5. Ibid., 3–4.

6. Martin Luther, *The Large Catechism*, trans. F. Bente and W. H. T. Dau (St. Louis: Concordia, 1921), 565–773.

7. James M. Kittelson, *Luther the Reformer: The Story of the Man and His Career* (Minneapolis: Augsburg, 1986), 222.

8. Ibid.

9. Martin Luther, *The Table Talk of Martin Luther*, ed. Alexander Chalmers and William Haslitt, Esq. (London: Bell & Daldy, 1872), 152–53.

10. Mark Galli, "From the Editor: The Forgotten Years of Martin Luther," *Christian History* 39 (1993), https://www.christianhistoryinstitute.org/magazine/article/forgotten-years-of-martin-luther/.

11. Rev. Heemann Fick, *The Life and Deeds of Martin Luther*, trans. Rev. Prof. M. Loy (Columbus, OH: J. A. Schulze, 1869), 131.

12. Kittelson, *Luther the Reformer*, 223.

13. Fick, *Life and Deeds*, 131.

14. Kittelson, *Luther the Reformer*, 223.

15. Fick, *Life and Deeds*, letter, Luther to Katie, October 4, 1529, 197.

Chapter 21

1. James M. Kittelson, *Luther the Reformer: The Story of the Man and His Career* (Minneapolis: Augsburg, 1986), 243–44 (last sentence).

2. Preserved Smith, PhD, *The Life and Letters of Martin Luther* (Boston and New York: Houghton Mifflin, 1911), 264.

3. Roland H. Bainton, *Here I Stand: A Life of Martin Luther*, Hendrickson Classic Biographies (Peabody, MA: Hendrickson, 2009 [1950]), 337.

4. Smith, *Life and Letters*, 251.

5. Ibid., 190.

6. Bainton, *Here I Stand*, 298.

7. Smith, *Life and Letters*, 353.

8. Bainton, *Here I Stand*, 307–8.

9. Kittelson, *Luther the Reformer*, 244.

10. Smith, *Life and Letters*, 369–70.

11. Ibid., 241.

12. Kittelson, *Luther the Reformer*, 261.

Chapter 22

1. James M. Kittelson, *Luther the Reformer: The Story of the Man and His Career* (Minneapolis: Augsburg, 1986), 272.

2. Ibid.

3. Roland H. Bainton, *Here I Stand: A Life of Martin Luther*, Hendrickson Classic Biographies (Peabody, MA: Hendrickson, 2009 [1950]), 298.

4. Kittelson, *Luther the Reformer*, 274 (said to Rosheim).

5. E. G. Schwiebert, *Luther and His Times: The Reformation from a New Perspective* (St. Louis: Concordia, 1950), 599.

Chapter 23

1. Preserved Smith, PhD, *The Life and Letters of Martin Luther* (Boston and New York: Houghton Mifflin, 1911), 353–54.

2. Ibid., 354.

3. Ibid.

4. Edwin P. Booth, *Martin Luther: The Great Reformer* (Uhrichsville, OH: Barbour and Co., 1995), 191.

5. James M. Kittelson, *Luther the Reformer: The Story of the Man and His Career* (Minneapolis: Augsburg, 1986), 282.

6. Ibid., 281.

7. Smith, *Life and Letters*, 417.

8. Ibid., 421.

9. Ibid., 422.

10. Ibid., 423.

11. Ibid.

12. Ibid.

Author's Note

1. James M. Kittelson, *Luther the Reformer: The Story of the Man and His Career* (Minneapolis: Augsburg, 1986), 190.

WORKS CONSULTED

Alex, Ben. *Martin Luther: The German Monk Who Changed the Church*. Heroes of Faith and Courage. Copenhagen: Scandinavia Publishing House, 1995.

Bainton, Roland H. *Here I Stand: A Life of Martin Luther*. Hendrickson Classic Biographies. Peabody, MA: Hendrickson, 2009 [1950].

———. *The Reformation of the Sixteenth Century*. Boston: Beacon Press, 1952. See esp. pp. 3–76.

Booth, Edwin P. *Martin Luther: The Great Reformer*. Uhrichsville, OH: Barbour, 1995.

Brown, Perry. "Preaching from the Print Shop." *Christian History* 34 (1992). https://www.christianhistoryinstitute.org/magazine/article/preaching-from-the-print-shop/.

———. "Profit-Hungry Printers." *Christian History* 34 (1992). https://www.christianhistoryinstitute.org/magazine/article/profit-hungry-printers/.

Cary, Phillip. "Luther: Gospel, Law, and Reformation." The Great Courses Lecture Series (CD/DVD/Streaming). Chantilly, VA: The Teaching Company, 2004.

Dillenberger, John, ed. *Martin Luther: Selections from His Writings*. New York: Doubleday, 1961.

Doak, Robin S. *Pope Leo X: Opponent of the Reformation.* Minneapolis: Compass Point, 2006.

Duffy, Eamon. *Saints and Sinners: A History of the Popes.* New Haven: Yale University Press, 2006. See esp. pp. 177–208.

Durant, Will. *The Reformation.* New York: Simon & Schuster, 1957. See esp. pp. 293–402.

Empires: Martin Luther. Cassian Harrison, director. 115 min. DVD. Arlington, VA: PBS Home Video, 2002.

Fearon, Mike. *Martin Luther.* Minneapolis: Bethany House, 1986.

Fick, Rev. Heemann. *The Life and Deeds of Martin Luther.* Trans. Rev. Prof. M. Loy. Columbus, OH: J. A. Schulze, 1869.

Flowers, Sarah. *The Reformation.* San Diego: Lucent Books, 1996.

Galli, Mark. "Martin Luther's Later Years: Did You Know?" *Christian History* 39 (1993). https://www.christian historyinstitute.org/magazine/article/martin-luthers -later-years-did-you-know/.

———. "The Weak Man Behind a Mighty Fortress." *Christian History* 39 (1993). https://www.christian historyinstitute.org/magazine/article/weak-man-behind -a-mighty-fortress/.

———. "The Decisive Documents of 1520." *Christian History* 34 (1992). https://www.christianhistoryinstitute.org /magazine/article/decisive-documents-of-1520/.

———. "Protestants' Most-Famous Document." *Christian History* 34 (1992). https://www.christianhistoryinstitute.org /magazine/article/protestants-most-famous-document/.

———. "From the Editor: Dwarfed by a Giant." *Christian History* 34 (1992). https://www.christianhistoryinstitute .org/magazine/article/dwarfed-by-a-giant/.

———. "From the Editor: The Forgotten Years of Martin Luther." *Christian History* 39 (1993). https://www .christianhistoryinstitute.org/magazine/article/forgotten -years-of-martin-luther/.

George, Timothy Dr. "Dr. Luther's Theology." *Christian History* 34 (1992). https://www.christianhistoryinstitute .org/magazine/article/dr-luthers-theology/.

Grant, George, and Gregory Wilbur. *The Christian Almanac.* Nashville: Cumberland House, 2004.

Gregory, Brad S. "The History of Christianity in the Reformation Era, Part 1." The Great Courses Lecture Series (DVD/CD/Streaming). Chantilly, VA: The Teaching Company, 2001.

Grime, Paul J. "Changing the Tempo of Worship." *Christian History* 39. https://www.christianhistoryinstitute.org /magazine/article/changing-the-tempo-of-worship/.

Gritsch, Eric W. "The Unrefined Reformer." *Christian History* 39 (1993). https://www.christianhistoryinstitute.org /magazine/article/luther-unrefined-reformer/.

———. "Was Luther Anti-Semitic?" *Christian History* 39 (1993). https://www.christianhistoryinstitute.org /magazine/article/was-luther-anti-semitic/.

Grun, Bernard. *The Timetables of History.* New York: Simon & Schuster, 1963.

Gyldenvand, Lily M. *Martin Luther: Giant of Faith.* Minneapolis: Augsburg, 1981.

Hendrix, Scott A. "Legends About Luther." *Christian History* 34 (1992). https://www.christianhistoryinstitute.org /magazine/article/legends-about-luther/.

Jacobsen, Herbert K. "Martin Luther's Early Years: Did You Know?" *Christian History* 34 (1992). https://www .christianhistoryinstitute.org/magazine/article/luthers -early-years-did-you-know/.

Jeffreys, Mary Ann. "Colorful Sayings of Colorful Luther." *Christian History* 34 (1992). https://www .christianhistoryinstitute.org/magazine/article/colorful -sayings-of-colorful-luther/.

Kittelson, James M. "The Accidental Revolutionary." *Christian History* 34 (1992). https://www.christianhistory institute.org/magazine/article/accidental-revolutionary/.

———. "The Breakthrough." *Christian History* 34 (1992). https://www.christianhistoryinstitute.org/magazine/ article/luthers-breakthrough/.

———. *Luther the Reformer: The Story of the Man and His Career.* Minneapolis: Augsburg, 1986.

———. "What Was Luther's World Like?" *Christian History* 34 (1992). https://www.christianhistoryinstitute.org /magazine/article/what-was-luthers-world-like/.

Klug, Eugene F. A. "Luther's Will and Testaments." *Christian History* 39 (1993). https://www.christianhistoryinstitute .org/magazine/article/luthers-will-and-testaments/.

Linder, Robert A. "Allies or Enemies?" *Christian History* 39 (1993): 40–44.

Luther, Martin. "Christianity for Common Folk." *Christian History* 39 (1993). https://www.christianhistoryinstitute .org/magazine/article/christianity-for-common-folk.

————. "Concerning Christian Liberty—1520." In *The Harvard Classics*, vol. 36, trans. R. S. Grignon, 353–97, New York: P. F. Collier & Son, 1910.

————. "Disputation of Doctor Martin Luther on the Power and Efficacy of Indulgences—1517." In *Works of Martin Luther*, vol. 1, trans. Adolph Spaeth, L. D. Reed, Henry Eyster Jacobs, et al., 29–38. Philadelphia: A. J. Holman Co., 1915.

————. "How I Pray." *Christian History* 39 (1993). https://www.christianhistoryinstitute.org/magazine/article/how-i-pray/.

————. *The Large Catechism.* In *Triglot Concordia: The Symbolical Books of the Evangelical Lutheran Church*, 565–773. Trans. F. Bente and W. H. T. Dau. St. Louis: Concordia, 1921.

————. *The Letters of Martin Luther.* Trans. Margaret A. Currie. London: Macmillan, 1908.

————. *Luther's Correspondence and Other Contemporary Letters*, vol. 1. Trans. and ed. Preserved Smith, PhD. Philadelphia: The Lutheran Publication Society, 1913.

————. "A Mighty Fortress Is Our God." Trans. Frederick H. Hedge. Hymn 67 in *The Methodist Hymnal*. Nashville: The Methodist Book Concern, 1939.

————. "Powerful Preaching." *Christian History* 39 (1993). https://www.christianhistoryinstitute.org/magazine/article/powerful-preaching/.

————. *A Short Exposition of Dr. Martin Luther's Small Catechism.* St. Louis: Concordia, 1912. See esp. pp. 1–8.

————. *The Table Talk of Martin Luther.* New ed., with *The Life of Martin Luther* by Alexander Chalmers. Trans.

and ed. William Hazlitt, Esq. London: Bell & Daldy, 1872. See esp. pp. 152–53.

MacCuish, Dolina. *Luther and His Katie*. Ross-shire, UK: Christian Focus Publications, 1999.

Marty, Martin E. "Luther's Living Legacy." Interview. *Christian History* 39 (1993). https://www.christianhistory institute.org/magazine/article/luthers-living-legacy/.

McGiffert, Arthur Cushman. *Martin Luther: The Man and His Work*. New York: Century Co., 1911.

N. A. "Confiteor." https://en.wikipedia.org/wiki/Confiteor.

N. A. "Martin Luther." *Catholic Encyclopedia*. http://www .newadvent.org/cathen/09438b.htm.

N. A. "Peasant's War." http://en.wikipedia.org/wiki/Peasants' _War.

Norwich, John Julius. *Absolute Monarchs: A History of the Papacy*. New York: Random House, 2011. See esp. pp. 275–98.

Oberman, Heiko A. "Fool in Rome." *Christian History* 34 (1992). https://www.christianhistoryinstitute.org/ magazine/article/fool-in-rome/.

O'Malley, John W., SJ. *A History of the Popes: From Peter to the Present*. Lanham, MD: Rowman & Littlefield, 2010. See esp. pp. 171–87.

Ozment, Steven. "Reinventing Family Life." *Christian History* 39 (1993). https://www.christianhistoryinstitute .org/magazine/article/reinventing-family-life/.

———. "A Monk Marries: Luther's Wit and Wisdom about His New Estate." *Christian History* 39 (1993). https://www.christianhistoryinstitute.org/magazine /article/a-monk-marries/.

Robbert, George S. "Martin Luther's Early Years: Recommended Resources." *Christian History* 34 (1992). https://www.christianhistoryinstitute.org/magazine/article/martin-luthers-early-years-recommended-resources/.

———. "Martin Luther's Later Years: Recommended Resources." *Christian History* 39 (1993). https://www.christianhistoryinstitute.org/magazine/article/luthers-later-years-recommended-resources/.

Robinson, James Harvey. *Readings in European History*, vol. 2. Boston: Ginn & Co., 1906.

Sanders, Ruth H. *German: Biography of a Language*. New York: Oxford University Press, 2010. See esp. pp. 117–56.

Schurb, Ken. "Martin Luther's Early Years: Christian History Timeline." *Christian History* 34 (1992). https://www.christianhistoryinstitute.org/magazine/article/martin-luthers-early-years-timeline/.

———. "Martin Luther's Later Years: Christian History Timeline." *Christian History* 39 (1993). https://www.christianhistoryinstitute.org/magazine/article/martin-luther-later-years-timeline/.

Schwiebert, E. G. *Luther and His Times: The Reformation from a New Perspective*. St. Louis: Concordia, 1950.

Smith, Preserved, PhD. *The Life and Letters of Martin Luther*. Boston and New York: Houghton Mifflin, 1914.

Spitz, Dr. Lewis W. "The Political Luther." *Christian History* 34 (1992). https://www.christianhistoryinstitute.org/magazine/article/political-luther/.

Thigpen, Paul. "Luther's Political Allies." *Christian History* 34 (1992). https://www.christianhistoryinstitute.org/magazine/article/luthers-political-allies/.

———. "Luther's Political Nemesis." *Christian History* 34 (1992). https://www.christianhistoryinstitute.org/magazine/article/luthers-political-nemesis/.

———. "Martin Luther's Early Years: A Gallery of Friends and Enemies." *Christian History* 34 (1992). https://www.christianhistoryinstitute.org/magazine/article/luther-gallery-of-friends-and-enemies/.

———. "Martin Luther's Later Years: A Gallery—Family Album." *Christian History* 39 (1993). https://www.christianhistoryinstitute.org/magazine/article/martin-luthers-gallery-family-album/.

———. "The Parents Luther Feared Disgracing." *Christian History* 34 (1992). https://www.christianhistoryinstitute.org/magazine/article/parents-luther-feared-disgracing/.

Tucker, Ruth A. *Parade of the Faith: A Biographical History of the Christian Church.* Grand Rapids: Zondervan, 2011. See esp. pp. 217–38.

Yonge, Charlotte Mary. *Cameos from English History: The Wars of the Roses.* Third Series. London: Macmillan, 1877. See esp. pp. 310–99.

Zecher, Henry. "The Bible Translation That Rocked the World." *Christian History* 34 (1992). https://www.christianhistoryinstitute.org/magazine/article/bible-translation-that-rocked-the-world/.